Temple Israel Library
Minneapolis, Minn.

———

Please sign your full name on the above
card.

Return books promptly to the Library or
Temple Office.

Fines will be charged for overdue books
or for damage or loss of same.

DEMCO

FINDING OURSELVES

FINDING OURSELVES

Sermons on the Art of Living

by

SIDNEY GREENBERG

Rabbi, Temple Sinai, Philadelphia, Pa.

JONATHAN DAVID
Publishers New York

FINDING OURSELVES

Copyright 1964, by Sidney Greenberg

Library of Congress Catalog Card No. 64-19751

PRINTED IN THE UNITED STATES OF AMERICA

TABLE OF CONTENTS

A WORD TO THE READER

ANY author who is familiar with Kohelet's weary complaint that "of the making of books there is no end," instinctively feels impelled to justify himself and his handiwork against the charge of the ancient cynic. Why indeed another book?

The author has to answer, too, to those who deprecate the sermon in general, and the Jewish sermon in particular. A substantial number of knowledgeable observers of the contemporary Jewish scene feel that the sermon should give way to the lecture and that the synagogue should take on more of the character of the classroom. Their question is naturally: Why another book of sermons?

Kohelet can be answered with relative ease. His unhappiness over the multiplicity of books did not prevent him from adding another. And it is fortunate for posterity that he was not inhibited. The Bible would be a poorer collection if he had taken his own admonition too seriously. One need not necessarily possess his literary gifts to follow his example. If only those birds sang who have the most beautiful voices, the forest would be almost silent.

Those who question the basic value of the sermon as a vehicle for instruction will admit that there are times when only the sermon will meet the demands of the occasion. They may not be able to agree with Herman Melville who declares in *Moby Dick*:

> "For the pulpit is ever the earth's foremost part,
> All the rest comes in its rear;
> The pulpit leads the world!"

They will not be able to deny however, that the modern Jew's need for emotional stimulation and spiritual inspiration is answered better through the medium of the sermon than by the lecture. This is especially true on the High Holy Days when so many of our people are present who do not attend services with any regularity throughout the year. The august character of these days demand themes of highest concern and most intimate application. Such themes are far more effectively treated in sermons. All but one of the sermons in this collection were, indeed, preached on the High Holy Days.

Much of the encouragement for the preparation of this volume was provided by my good friends of Temple Sinai upon whom I also threw much of the blame for my earlier collection of sermons, *Adding Life to Our Years.* What I wrote in the preface to that book is no less true of this one. "Chief among my reasons for publishing these sermons have been the repeated requests of my congregants for written copies of sermons which had made a special impact upon them. In a very real sense these sermons are as much their property as mine. Their needs have served as my motivations. Their predicaments have been my texts. From the crucible of their experience I have distilled my themes. By their constant loyalty they have provided me with the utmost stimulation to search for answers commensurate with the earnestness of their questions. Thus they have been much more than passive listeners to these sermons. They have almost literally drawn them out of me. Their right to these sermons can, therefore, neither be contested nor denied. This book enables me to acknowledge their claim and to attempt to satisfy it." I wish I could offer them a more ample reward for being my patient audience for twenty-one years.

I was also more than a little motivated to publish this collection of sermons by the most generous reactions of my colleagues in the Orthodox, Conservative and Reform rabbinate to my first volume of sermons. Their unsolicited words of praise were dramatic reminders of how deep is our need for constant exchange of insights and ideas. Their letters also indicated, incidentally, that the sermon is treated with utmost earnestness by the American rabbi of all denominations. I know only too well how numerous and how varied are the demands made upon the rabbi's time and energies; with what marginal resources he must too often confront the onerous task and fierce discipline of sermon preparation. It is my sincere hope that he may find some help in the efforts of another toiler in the vineyard.

No one is more sensitive than I to the inadequacies of these sermons. It does require more than average audacity to commit any word to the awesome finality of the printed page. Frank Lloyd Wright once pointed out that an architect who makes a mistake can always urge his clients to grow ivy on the walls but what refuge is available to the author? In moments when trepidation lays siege to my spirits, I take heart from the knowledge that I am part of a mighty company. Such at least is the reassurance provided by James S. Stewart in his *Heralds of God*: "No man knows how to preach. You will have to reckon with this significant, disconcerting fact, that the greatest preachers who have ever lived have confessed themselves poor bunglers to the end, groping after an ideal which eluded them forever. When you have been preaching for twenty years, you will be beginning to realize how incalculably much there is to learn. There will be days when the Socratic knowledge of your ignorance will desolate and overwhelm you. Even if Providence should spare you to this work for fifty years, your thought will be, as the gloaming closes in around you, 'If only I could start all over again now!' "

This book is by no means designed to serve as a model of preaching. Rather is it intended to record the efforts of one rabbi to draw out of the rich heritage of a proud and ancient faith the sustenance to nourish the lean spirits of a generation of Jews who have great need for the extravagant wealth which past generations have bequeathed to them. Most of the sermons are of a personal nature and speak of the intimate concerns that weigh upon our hearts. I believe that Judaism has a great deal to say to us as individuals, that it has much inspired counsel to offer and that, in an age of vast confusion and uncertainty, it can contribute impressively to help each of us in the sacred and inescapable task of *Finding Ourselves*—as human beings, as Jews, as children of God.

This book is offered as a token of abiding gratitude to Him who, in the words of our Prayer Book "mercifully endows man with knowledge and teaches mortals understanding."

SIDNEY GREENBERG

TEMPLE SINAI
APRIL 14, 1964
2 IYAR, 5724

FINDING OURSELVES

ARE WE OUTLIVING OURSELVES?

One mark of man's greatness is his ability to live on after he has died. One serious danger which confronts him is the possibility of dying while he is still alive. Some years ago one religious sect took as its motto these words: "Millions now living will never die." Whereupon some one commented: "That may be so. But the tragedy is that millions now living are already dead and don't know it." Are we staying alive all our lives?

Preached on Kol Nidre, 1955

1

Are We Outliving Ourselves?

A FEW YEARS AGO when Yom Kippur coincided with September 29th in the English calendar, the window of a Jewish shop-keeper in London displayed the following somewhat ambiguous notice: "Closed all day Monday, September 29 for annual stock-taking." Well, we are going to be open during the better part of the next twenty-four hours for our collective annual stock-taking. And when we start probing within, as we already have in our Kol Nidre liturgy, we are concerned not so much with what we have as with what we lack.

In J. P. Marquand's novel, *Point of No Return*, there is a sharply pointed comment made about the principal character. It is said of him, "He knew all the little answers but he missed the large questions." He knew the little answers—how to keep advancing himself on his job, how to make life comfortable—but he missed the big questions: What is the purpose of life? How can it be made meaningful? What does it all add up to?

We live at a time when the ability to give the little answers can be very remunerative. One television program which is currently raising the blood pressure of all America and is inducing nervous twitches in its participants offers as much as $64,000 for some of the little answers. In less dramatic fashion, so much of our daily living is devoted to the little answers. What shall I wear today? What movie shall we see tonight? What shall I prepare for dinner? These are typical of our ordinary pedestrian concerns. But what of the truly larger questions that go to the very core

3

of the human enterprise? Yom Kippur is deeply concerned with them.

Tonight I should like to direct our attention to a question suggested by one of the saddest lines a man ever wrote about himself. The writer was the great 19th century poet, Lord Byron, whose poetic genius was in sharp contrast to his woefully dissolute character. His untamed passions precipitated his untimely death at the age of thirty-six, but even before then he summed up his personal tragedy in a self-indictment which was remarkable both for its insight and its frankness. "I have outlived myself," he wrote, "by many a year."

At first blush this sounds like a fantastic statement but it was frightfully true. Byron was perceptive enough to realize that he had lived on after the best in him had died.

To be sure, Byron represents an extreme case of moral collapse. Yet Byron's bold self-appraisal underscores one of life's most dreary possibilities. We human beings who are capable of living on after we have died are also liable to die while we are still alive. This, I take it, is the true meaning of the oft-quoted rabbinic paradox: "The righteous even after death are alive. The wicked even while they live are dead." This affliction, however, is not limited only to the wicked.

We can live perfectly harmless lives, bothering no one, violating no laws of society, inflicting no hurt, and yet commit the great sin against ourselves by outliving ourselves. That we are prone to do so more often than we suspect is indicated by the frequency with which this theme recurs in the writings of life's most careful observers. We have already heard from our sages on this score. Listen to Stephen Vincent Benet:

> Life is not lost by dying.
> Life is lost minute by minute, day by dragging day,
> In all the thousand small uncaring ways.

ARE WE OUTLIVING OURSELVES?

Listen to one of the most kindly and dedicated spirits of our time, Dr. Albert Schweitzer: "The tragedy of life is not . . . in the fact of death itself. The tragedy of life is what dies inside a man while he lives."

Let us then each of us ask of ourselves tonight the big question: Are we outliving ourselves?

To help us in our probing, let us break down our big question into three more specific ones which I believe touch on those sensitive areas of life which are most perishable.

Let us ask in the first place: Have we outlived our ideals and our dreams?

Dr. Albert Schweitzer, whom we quoted a moment ago, has penetratingly described the sad process by which we shake off the lovely buds which flower on our youthful tree of life. One of the glorious characteristics of youth is its capacity for bold dreams, its ability to believe in the good and the true and the beautiful. But as we grow older we tend to imitate the weary and the cynical adults, and we shed the high resolves and noble dreams which set us aflame in our tender years. Dr. Schweitzer describes the process:

"We believed once in the victory of truth; but we do not now. We believed in goodness; we do not now. We were zealous for justice, but we are not so now. We trusted in the power of kindness, peaceableness; we do not now. We were capable of enthusiasm, but we are not so now. To get through the shoals and storms of life more easily we have lightened our craft, throwing overboard what we thought could be spared. But it was really our stock of food and drink of which we deprived ourselves; our craft is now easier to manage but we ourselves are in a decline."

It would be most instructive for all of us and very humbling for many of us, if we compared our goals today with the ideals we cherished ten or twenty years ago. How many lives have suffered a progressive deterioration of motive, a gradual contraction of purpose and shrinking of the horizons?

How many of us went forth in our chosen vocations dedicated to justice and then decided to play it safe?

How many of us swore in our youthful hearts that we would try to heal the hurt of humanity only to find ourselves preoccupied exclusively with our own comforts and luxuries?

How many of us stood on the threshold of parenthood and vowed that we would execute faithfully the sacred responsibility it confers only to become absentee parents who give our children everything except what they need most, ourselves?

How many of us promised ourselves that when we had more time, when life's economic demands would become less insistent, we would take seriously our obligations as Jews? We would read, we would attend adult classes, we would lend a hand in communal endeavors, we would take our children to the finest place a parent can take a child—to synagogue services. Then we came upon more leisure than Jews have ever had, we became more comfortable than a Jewish community has ever been and we decided to invest our added time and resources exclusively in amusement, recreation and self-delight.

There is a melancholy anecdote concerning two little girls in Nazi Germany. Each thought herself to be a pure Aryan. When they became more intimately acquainted, one confided that she had a Jewish grandmother. "That's strange," said the second one, "I have a Jewish grandmother too."

The first thought for a moment and said: "I know what it is. That's what happens to people as they become older. They turn into Jews."

Well, many promised ourselves in our younger years that as we grew older we would turn into better Jews. But do the advancing years find us growing closer or drifting further away?

How many of us have become so preoccupied with immediates that we have lost sight of ultimates, so that George Eliot's description of Silas Marner might well apply to us too: "His life had reduced itself to the mere functions of weaving and hoarding without a contemplation of an end towards which these functions tended. So year after year Silas Marner had lived in this solitude, his guineas rising in the iron pot, and his life narrowing and hardening itself more and more into a mere pulsation of desire and satisfaction, which had no relation to any other being."

Here then is a big question indeed for each of us: Have we outlived our dreams and our ideals?

Dr. Schweitzer advises us: "The great secret of success is to go through life as a man who never gets used up. Grow into your ideals so that life can never rob you of them." Yes, that is the secret of successful living, not in the sense that the popular slogans and catch-phrases of our commercial society envision it, but as it is seen by people who hold life sacred and look upon man as a creature of infinite potentialities. For what after all is our uniquely human endowment? Our will to live? Scarcely! The horse also wants to live. Our preeminence over the beast is that we want to live a maximum life. We can become possessed by a dream, enslaved by an ideal and we can go through life without getting used up.

When we return the Torah to the Ark we pray, chadesh yamaynu k'kedem—"Renew our days as of old." Against the background of what we have been saying this becomes one of our most urgent needs. We need to renew the high resolves and deep yearnings of old if we are not to outlive our own grandest aspirations. And the message of our tradition is that this prayer can be answered. The lesson of the lives of the great souls of Jewish history is that this prayer has been answered.

> "Ah, great it is to believe the dream
> As we stand in youth by the starry stream,
> But a greater thing is to fight life through
> And to say at the end, the dream is true."

7

Let us proceed now to our second question which I would put as follows: Have we outlived our appreciation for the commonplace blessings of life?

The importance of holding on to our youthful sense of wonder and enthusiasm at the sheer glory of living, is so obvious that I hesitated to deal with it tonight. But the longer I go on observing life, the more convinced do I become that the true function of the pulpit is not so much to elucidate the obscure as it is to emphasize the obvious.

A bold fact of our daily lives is that they are too often untouched by an appreciation for the countless blessings close at hand precisely because they are so close at hand. Much of the prevailing tension in our personal lives issues from our inability to find satisfaction in our already abundant possessions. Much of our chasing after excitement and thrills is rooted in our failure to find contentment in the more placid joys of life. Much of the wearying monotony and insipid taste of our daily routine stem from our failure to behold in each day a never-ending succession of God's unfolding kindnesses. And if we have outlived this gratefulness for life's bounty, have we not left behind life's most tasty ingredient? For is not the City of Contentment, as someone said, located in the State of Mind?

Do you recall what Emily says in Thornton Wilder's drama *Our Town?* You remember that after her death Emily is permitted to relive a day of her childhood. When she does so, she realizes how badly she failed to appreciate its beauty and the significance of life. "It goes so fast. We don't have time to look at one another. . . . I didn't realize. . . . So all that was going on and we never noticed. . . . One more look. . . . Good-by. . . . Good-by Grover's Corners. . . . Mama and Papa. . . . Good-by to clocks ticking . . . and Mama's sunflowers. . . . And food and coffee. And new ironed dresses and hot baths . . . and sleeping and waking up. Oh, Earth, you're too wonderful for anybody to realize you. Do any human beings ever realize life while they live it?—Every, every minute."

Some of us must travel half way around the globe before we discover the beauty of our homes and the blessing of the familiar faces. Others must become physically stricken before we know the glory of walking, and feeding ourselves. Still others must be threatened with the loss of loved ones before we appreciate their sustaining influence in our lives. And almost all of us must see the threatening fist of the conqueror before we wake up to the privileges of freedom and equality which are the American heritage.

But Judaism has a simpler prescription for keeping alive a sense of gratefulness. That is the way of prayer. To most of us, prayer is synonymous with petition. We are moved to pray only when we want something very badly—the recovery of a loved one, a year of life and sustenance for our families, escape from immanent danger. If we examine our prayer-book carefully, however, we will find that so much of it is a catalogue of life's blessings whose daily recitation is designed to impress upon us the inexhaustible wealth with which a merciful God has endowed us. The Jew who has prayed thoughtfully in the morning has been reminded, among other things, of the joy of waking up, the boon of being free, the blessing of sight, the privilege of being a moral creature, the miracle of the human body, the benediction of being under the benevolent care of God who clothes us, guides us, gives us strength when we are weary and "who hast provided for all my needs." This mood of gratefulness runs throughout our prayerbook and in the heart of the Jew who uses it, it puts a magnet which as it sweeps through the hours finds in every one of them particles of mercy and blessing. How easy it becomes for him to sing with the poet:

> For all that God in mercy sends
> For health and children, home and friends
> For comfort in the time of need

For every kindly word and deed
For happy thoughts and holy talk
For everything give thanks!

For sweet sleep which comes with night
For the returning morning's light
For the bright sun that shines on high
For the stars glittering in the sky
For these and everything we see
O Lord, our hearts we lift to Thee
For everything give thanks.
—(*Helen Isabella Tupper*)

For the last, I have left the most important question of all: Have we outlived our belief in God?

The newspaper reported an amusing and instructive coincidence a little while ago. In a little town in Minnesota three ministers posted the titles of their Sunday morning sermons on their respective bulletin boards. And as one walked through the town, these are the titles he read in order:

Where Is He?
He Is Here.
God Changes His Address.

As this item caught my eye, it occurred to me that this is the sad sequence that modern man has followed in his religious development. As a child he was full of questions about God. What is God like? Why can't I see God? If I close my room can God still get in? Where is He?

The questioning stage gave way to certainty. The growing child was most receptive to a belief in God, when it was sympathetically presented. He then felt with assurance: "He Is Here."

But somehow as he grew older, his certainty left him and if God did in fact exist, He was no longer too close, for God had changed His address.

Now this seems like a strange thing to talk about to Jews who have come to synagogue on Kol Nidre to pray. Surely if anyone believes in God, he would be the synagogue Jew. And I suppose if we were to ask for a show of hands now, God would get a rather substantial vote.

But I often wonder just how vital and significant this belief in God is to us. Does it really make a difference in our lives or is it similar, say, to our belief that the world is round? Interesting, of some consequence to map makers, pilots and ship captains, but of no real relevance to our daily doings. Is it what Coleridge might have called "a bed-ridden truth which lies asleep in the dormitories of our minds?"

Do we believe in the God of Micah who makes demands of us in our places of business, in our dealings with our fellow man: "What doth the Lord thy God require of thee, to do justice, to love mercy, to walk humbly with thy God?"

Do we believe in a God who is not remote, but who as the Psalmist says: "Is near to all who call upon Him, to all who call upon Him in truth?"

Do we believe in God even when He has prospered us so that we say "For it is from Thy hand that we have all?"

If we have outlived that kind of dynamic belief in God, if as far as we are concerned God has changed His address, has not something of greatest importance gone out of our lives?

One of the leading religious spokesmen of our time, has put it this way: "Whoever discards religious faith should appoint a day of mourning for his soul, and put on sack-cloth and ashes. He must take from his life the greatest thought that man the thinker ever had; the finest faith that man the worker ever leaned on, the surest help that man the sinner ever found, the strongest reliance that man the sufferer ever trusted in; the loftiest vision that man the lover ever saw, the only hope that man the mortal ever had."

An atheist has been defined as one "without invisible means

11

of support." If life is to stand under the tremendous pressures that weigh down upon it, if it is to be filled with a sense of worthwhileness and beauty, we need invisible means of support. We must recapture the conviction that God has not changed His address.

A charming and suggestive Midrash pictures the heavenly angels asking the Almighty when the New Year will begin. The Almighty however refuses to answer. "Why do you ask Me? Go down and ask My children." In a very real sense each of us determines when the New Year truly begins. It begins when a man or a woman begins to ask the big questions. A New Year dawns in its glory and splendor when the big questions are accompanied by the resolve to provide the big answers.

Dear friends, when will the New Year begin for you? The angels are waiting for your answer.

THE ART OF HOLDING ON

Life is a stern master who is forever teaching us the heavy duty
of relinquishing prized possessions. But there are certain possessions we must never surrender. What are they? How are we
to hold on to them?

Preached on Yom Kippur, 1955

2

The Art of Holding On

THIS MORNING'S sermon might be titled, "A Post-script to a Sermon," because it began as an annoying after-thought to the theme we considered last night.* After I had developed the theme that Judaism bids us not to outlive our uniquely human endowments, our high ideals, our constant gratefulness for our manifold blessings, our faith in God, my thoughts turned to this Yizkor hour. As I did so some gnawing questions began to assail me.

It is all well and good for me to speak of not outliving ourselves but how about the inescapable fact of life, of which Yizkor is a poignant reminder, that we do outlive loved ones? It is well perhaps to be reminded of the importance of holding on but what are we to do when life compels us to let go? I ask that we cherish life and yet Socrates correctly defined life "a persuader of death," a stern master who teaches us the heavy duty of relinquishing. Life not only demands retention of precious equipment; with equal insistence it compels the renunciation of prized possessions.

I needed only to compare our Temple Sinai family of today with what it was last Yom Kippur to realize that our little segment of humanity has paid a high toll during the last twelve months on the bridge of human frailty. Comrades have vanished from our sight "seized by the silent orders of omnipotent death," leaving behind aches and loneliness. Others have been visited by illness and disease which have left in their wake shrunken possibilities, weakened powers, restricted activities. Still others have known the anguish of blasted hopes, broken homes, betrayed hearts.

---

* Cf. "Are We Outliving Ourselves."

I plead that we hold on tenaciously to life and yet life has a way of loosening our grip and compelling us to yield treasures we are so reluctant to surrender.

The more these haunting questions disturbed me, the sharper did they become. I realized as I pondered them that it was precisely the loss of these cherished possessions which we must outlive which often induces us to surrender the noble possessions I said we ought not to outlive.

Our belief in life's possibilities and worthwhileness is pulverized by the death of one around whom and with whom we had erected the structure of our life's ideals. "The eager fate which carried thee took the better part of me." Our sense of gratefulness for life's blessings is severely dulled by the disappearance of our health or loved ones, the major sources of our blessings and gratitude.

And our belief in a loving God is highly vulnerable, as all of us know, to the assault of brutal facts. Many a ship of faith sails along serenely enough on an untroubled sea only to flounder on the rock of adversity.

It would seem that when we do surrender life's precious equipment whose retention I had urged, we often do so at the point of a gun held by the grim hand of misfortune.

This then was the disturbing dilemma which confronted me. How to reconcile the points I had labored to establish with the counterpoints which would not be silenced. For some days I was probably more difficult to live with than I usually am. For some agonizing hours I even contemplated the possibility of tearing up last night's sermon, which in retrospect may strike some of you as having been a rather inspired thought at that.

But last night's theme was too basic to Judaism's entire outlook on life to be discarded. And so I stayed with it a little longer until the light mercifully broke through. It was then that I realized that the questions which were gnawing at me did not in-

16

validate our thesis but on the contrary affirmed it and demanded a further extension of it. For while it is true that life's battering storms shake our ideals, undermine our sense of gratitude and threaten to engulf our faith, it is exactly in such moments that we most desperately must hold on to all three. For Cervantes spoke the profound truth when he said: "He who loses wealth loses much. He who loses a friend loses more. But he who loses his courage loses all." When life deprives us of the possessions we must outlive, it then becomes a thousandfold more important that we hold fast to the things we dare not outlive.

Let us now retrace our steps and consider once more the three possessions Judaism urges us to retain in the midst of the storm even more than in the calm hours.

The first is our belief in life's worthwhileness and in our ability to add to the sum of its goodness and beauty. Now what happens to us when one of our main props is kicked out from under us? Well, we have two choices.

One way is indicated by the bride in Charles Dickens' *Great Expectations*. Her groom disappears on their wedding day and at that point her life stops. Throughout the bitter years that drag wearily on, she continues to wear her wedding gown which becomes as it were a shroud in which her hope, her love, her zest for life are interred.

The same type of reaction under different circumstances is described by Stephen Graham in one of his stories. He tells of a poor Russian peasant woman who is found, long after her husband's death, clutching at the earth around his grave, pleading with him to come back because she needs him, his children need him and she cannot go on without him.

There is another type of reaction. I want you to listen to what Beethoven wrote in his will which he drew up at the age of thirty two. Life had inflicted upon him what was for him an especially bitter burden: "For six years I have been a hopeless case, cheated year by year by the hope of improvement. I am deaf. How can I endure an infirmity in the one sense which should have been more perfect than in others? . . . A little more and I would have put an end to my life—this wretched existence." With a burst of feeling he adds: "O Providence, grant me at last one day of pure joy; it has been so long since real joy echoed in my heart." Thus he wrote in 1802.

The time is now twenty four years later. The place is a theatre in Vienna. A wildly applauding audience is standing on its feet hailing the composer of the Ninth Symphony which was just performed for the first time. It has concluded with the chorus singing and the orchestra's playing of the composer's version of Schiller's Ode To Joy, a melodic crescendo of exuberance. As Beethoven stands there silently and turns the pages of his score, he can not hear a single sound of their huge ovation.

He whom life had maimed and moved to bitter protest has created a symphony whose joy still echoes in our hearts. His deafness had not been cured. It had only become more complete. But Beethoven had refused to give up his belief that he could continue to create, to write music, to enrich the treasury of the world's beauty.

We have dipped into literature and history to discover the possibilities which confront us all in the heavy hours. But we need not look into books to illustrate our choice. You and I know people who have come up with one response or the other. Can there be any doubt which one spells defeat and which one spells victory? Jewish custom dictates that the kriyah be made in the garment of the mourner while he is standing up—standing erect ready to move ahead, aware of life's duties yet alive to its continued possibilities. When we return from the cemetery we drink l'chayim—to life—that is the signpost to healing, to hope, to heroic achievement.

18

And what becomes of our sense of gratitude for life's blessings when a big blessing is withdrawn?

Here again we have to choose between one of two responses. We can become bitter and succumb to a wave of self-pity. We can feel so terribly sorry for ourselves. We can hurl our curses at life and give way to a mood of rebellion. We can imitate those of whom Charles Slattery said: "Like children they are, who when sent to bed go because they must, but as they climb the stairs nastily kick each stair by way of angry protest." We have all known such people and we soon find reasons for not phoning them or dropping by.

And then there are others, the glory of the human race, who know that while life can rob us of a loved one it cannot take from us the remembrance of the years we spent together and the lasting blessings the past years deposited with us. It is they who say of a loved one, as Georgia Harkness said of her father: "To know this life was good, it left its mark on me. Its work stands fast."

This same mood of gratefulness was captured by William Allen White in the face of life's most devastating loss, the death of his gifted daughter Mary. Writing to a friend who sent him a message of sympathy, he said:

"Mrs. White and I are standing on our feet, realizing that the loss is heavy and the blow is hard but not beating our hands against the bars and asking why. On our books Mary is a net gain. She was worth so much more than she cost and she left so much more behind than she took away that we are flooded with joyous memories and cannot question either the goodness of God or the general decency of man."

I think now also of Reuben Avinoam, whose name means "the father of Noam." Noam fell in Israel's War of Liberation in 1948. After the week of Shiva, his father wrote a moving Hebrew poem entitled, *Al Kayn Nodeh L'cho Eloha*, "Therefore, We Thank Thee God."

19

May I be permitted to quote only one stanza of it:

> For pleasant years,
> For one and twenty years
> Wherein Thou didst honor us with him, lent him to us
> For his steps walking humbly by our side on the little
>   isle of life:
> Years sown with the peace of his being,
> When like a gliding swan he made his way erect with
>   grace;
> Years shining with smiles
> Which like sun rays he spread around him,
> With good-hearted whispers, pardons by concession and
>   understanding
> Years shining with the light of his two eyes.
> Where dreams yearned, mingled with the sorrow of fate,
> Having a pure look and upright before God and man
> For this little gift,
> For 21 years full of life Thou gavest him and us,
> We thank Thee.

This is how we fulfil the command of our tradition which urges that we ought to thank God in the hour of trouble no less than in the hour of blessing.

Yes, deep within your soul and mine are huge resources for gratitude which we can tap in the hour of bereavement, and when we do so they release a stream of healing and hope which, while it cannot wash away our loss, can and does wash away bitterness and despair. It makes it possible for us to go on with courage and high resolve. It helps us to realize that, sad as it is to lose a loved one, it is sadder by far not to have had a loved one to lose, never to have been touched and enriched by the blessings of shared joy and love.

We come now to what is undoubtedly the most difficult possession to hold on to in the time of trouble, our faith in God. It is comparatively easy to say "The Lord is my Shepherd" when

"He maketh me to lie down in green pastures," but it is quite another matter when "I walk through the valley of the shadow of death." How many are capable of saying with the Psalmist even then: "Thou art with me"?

One of the most difficult letters I ever received came to me from a woman who did not know me, but who felt the need of pouring out her heavy heart to some one. When she read the announcement of the publication *A Treasury of Comfort*, she felt that here was someone interested in human grief and she proceeded to unburden herself. She wrote with deep tenderness and sensitivity. Her only brother, age 32, had been killed in an automobile accident. She dwelt at length on his many virtues. He was a lawyer of great promise, a human being infinitely good, modest and kind.

"It is most difficult to describe," she said, "what we went through and the extreme cruelty and injustice of his passing. . . . I am not an agnostic, but how can we believe in a Supreme Being when such a worthy and young life is taken for no reason at all?"

I do not have a copy of the answer I sent this woman because I wrote it by hand in the stillness of that night. But I remember that I answered in part by quoting from John Greenleaf Whittier's "Trust":

> The same old baffling questions! O my friend
> I can not answer them. . . .
> I have no answer for myself or thee,
> Save that I learned beside my mother's knee:
> 'All is of God that is, and is to be;
> And God is good.' Let this suffice us still,
> Resting in childlike trust upon His will
> Who moves to His great ends unthwarted by the ill.

This answer of the poet at least has the virtue of honesty. No one can claim to have a direct line to the Almighty. And perhaps it is in the essence of our belief in God that we cannot understand Him, for if we did He would cease being Infinite and become finite like ourselves. Just as an ant cannot climb into the mind of a man and hope to understand it, so can man not hope to understand the mind of God.

> "For My thoughts are not your thoughts,
> Neither are your ways My ways, saith the Lord.
> For as the heavens are higher than the earth,
> So are My ways higher than your ways,
> And My thoughts than your thoughts."

The complete answer must forever elude us. We can, however, proceed a little further towards the answer. When our faith is challenged perhaps we need a larger faith than the one we learned at mother's knee. After all, we were only children then and how much could mother expect us to understand? Too often what poses as faith is illusion. We believe in a God who is supposed to grant us and our loved ones special immunity and exemption against the ravages of life. Death on the highways can claim others' brothers but not ours; cancer may invade the bodies of others but not ours; floods may wipe out the life's toil of others but not ours. When the hour of anguish strikes we are ready to surrender what we thought was our faith. If we were wise, we would leave behind our illusions and struggle on to a higher faith.

Yes, dear unknown friend, you find it desperately difficult to believe in God because of your brother's death. But if you negate God how do you explain your brother's life? Whence came his passion to be of service to his fellow man, from what source flowed his great goodness, his humility, his kindness? Whence came that love that bound you together in a tie stronger than death? Could there be all this loveliness in his life unless it issued from a Greater Source outside of his life, any more than there could be light in the lamp by which I write if there were not a powerhouse which is sending the light?

If there were no God, why would you and I be trying so desperately to find Him and understand Him? I cannot believe that you and I in our most serious hours have been chasing shadows. You and I are looking for God because in our heart of hearts we know that He exists and He is waiting for us to find Him.

And one thing more, dear friend. Losing your brother was bitter, but if you compound your loss by surrendering your faith, what hope abides? For it is "faith which draws the poison from every grief, takes the sting from every loss, and quenches the fire of every pain; and only faith can do it."

In closing I would leave with you the healing prescription of a wise man who said: "Have courage for the great sorrows of life and patience for the small ones; and when you have laboriously accomplished your daily task, go to sleep in peace. God is awake."

At this point, dear friends, this sermon could end, but if I may I should like to add a postscript to a postscript, what we used to call P.P.S. at the foot of the letter. In this postscript we may find, as in many a young girl's letter, the most important line of all.

I have been pleading that we do not permit life's big losses to rob us of our great values. But I will not have done full justice to our human capacities if I did not go on to add that many of us never discover life's great values until we have had a big loss. It is one of life's astonishing paradoxes that we often see more clearly when our eyes have been dimmed by tears. In the soil of sorrow there often grow the tender shoots of compassion and sympathy and service. It often takes suffering to understand suffering. "A deep distress," said Wordsworth, "hath humanized my soul." Those who have sustained a great loss are often moved to take inventory into the manifold blessings that remain and thus become more grateful for their remaining treasures than they were when they were more abundantly endowed. And many a man who labors under the illusion of self-sufficiency becomes aware of his

23

dependence upon God only when he has been humbled by a heavy burden. Like Chateaubriand, the unbeliever, after the death of his sister, he might say: "I wept and then I believed."

We human beings, it appears, can do more than endure losses. We can use them to greater ends.

In Israel we saw a rare cactus plant on which there grows an exquisitely lovely flower. That flower is called "Malkat Halielah" —Queen of the Night—because it has the strange characteristic of blooming only in the darkest part of the night. When the blackness is deepest, the Malkat Halielah comes bursting out. You and I can be like her and in the dark night of sorrow shine forth robed in our full human splendor, bedecked in all our God-given glory.

THE ART OF WAITING

A candidate for the police force was asked: "If you were alone in a police car and were pursued by a gang of desperate criminals in another car doing forty miles an hour along a lonely road, what would you do?" Without a moment's hesitation the candidate replied: "Fifty."

Not all of life's problems are solved by greater speed. Some require a knowledge of how to wait. But waiting is not always a virtue either.

Preached on Rosh Hashanah, 1963

3

The Art of Waiting

THE HIGH HOLY DAY prayer book, like the prayer book which we use throughout the year, is filled not only with great petitions but even more, with great affirmations. It is not only a book for asking; it is also a book for declaring. As we pray we rehearse our beliefs about man's place in God's world, the destiny of man himself and the nature of his Creator. And it is to one particular attribute of God that I should like to call special attention today.

On each of the High Holy Days the recitation of *Unsaneh Tokef* is followed by this prayer: "Thou art slow to anger and ready to forgive. Thou desirest not the death of the sinner but that he return from his evil way and live. Even until his dying day Thou waitest for him. If he repents, Thou wilt immediately receive him." God waits for man to repent. God is a God who waits.

When we stop to reflect on this, it is a rather striking thought. We usually think of God who does things promptly and swiftly. He has only to will and things happen. But the prayer book reminds us that this is not so, that even when God wants very much for something to happen, He has to wait. However much He desires that we live with justice and righteousness and compassion, He must wait until you and I choose to live in this way.

The more we understand the world in which we live, the more impressive becomes the evidence that God is a God who waits. In less sophisticated days it was generally believed that when God wanted man to appear, He simply mixed a few elements and before the sun had set, man had arisen. Today we know otherwise.

Slowly, painfully, over unnumbered millions of years man evolved out of the primeval slime until he could stand erect and look towards the heavens. God was in no hurry when He made man. First, He fashioned the impulse to life in a one celled protozoa and then He waited.

Wherever we look we find very little evidence that God was ever in a great hurry. On the contrary, everything we see indicates patience and planning and waiting. The most delicate flower, the sturdiest tree, the tallest mountain, each testifies in its own eloquent way that God knows how to wait.

As we read the remarkable history of our people we notice some of this Divine patience reflected in it. Henrik Ibsen, the great Danish playwright, once said that the Jews taught him "how to wait." They were driven into Babylonian exile and instead of despairing, they waited—waited for decades until the day when they could do what no other people had ever done—go back to the land whence they had been driven. Several centuries later, they went into exile a second time. Their broken fragments were scattered in every land of the globe. Again they waited—waited for nineteen harsh centuries to be restored to the land which lived in their memories, their rituals, their prayers and their hopes. What a remarkable capacity to wait! Long, long ago our people affirmed its faith in the day when nations shall beat their swords into plowshares and their spears into pruning hooks, a day when the earth would be covered with justice as the waters cover the sea. And while they saw little evidence of either peace or justice they reaffirmed their faith in the coming of these things and they waited. En route to the gas chambers and the crematoria they repeated Maimonides' article of faith, "I believe in the coming of the Messiah and even though he tarry, nevertheless I will wait for him. I will wait for his coming any day." We are a people which has learned supremely the lesson of the Divine, of waiting and hoping without getting tired of waiting or surrendering our hopes.

Each of us as human beings needs large quantities of this ability to wait. Christopher Morley once said that whenever he saw a telephone receiver it reminded him of the many people who are waiting to hear some crucial news over that telephone. A message spelling life or death, and for some young girls, romance and love. So much of our lives is spent waiting. We wait for ambitions to be fulfilled and dreams to be realized. We wait for loved ones to come back and for the long, hard winter to pass. We wait for evil to be crushed and goodness to be vindicated. We wait for our hurts to be healed and our sorrows to be softened. "He that can have patience," said Benjamin Franklin, "can have what he wills." We must learn how to wait.

This is not a popular doctrine in our time. We are addicted to speed. "Instant" is a key-word in our vocabulary. A recent magazine article which dealt with new methods of freeze-drying foods so that it would be possible to eat complete meals years after they had been prepared, concluded with this statement: "The housewife has already accepted instant coffee, instant pie mixes and so on. Why not instant everything?" Indeed, why not instant everything? One of my favorite ladies in the cartoon world was recently shown examining a jar of coffee in the supermarket and she says, "I think it's misleading to call it instant coffee when you still have to boil the water."

A recent *New York Times* dispatch quotes a West German professor, a specialist in the problem of alcoholism, who studied the drinking habits in the Soviet Union and concluded that the Russians drank as though their aim was "instant drunkenness." One shrewd observer of the contemporary scene calls attention to some of the verbs we use to describe our daily actions: We *leap* out of bed, we *gulp* our coffee, we *bolt* our food, we *whiz* into town, we *dash* to the office, we *tear* for home and we *drop* dead. This is a generation which wants what it wants when it wants it. We want it yesterday, today at the very latest, certainly not tomorrow. We have become worshippers of the goddess of speed. We become impatient if we miss one section of a revolving door. Knowing how to wait is not one of our conspicuous qualities.

And that is why we have to be reminded that God is a God who waits. We are descendants of a people which taught humanity how to wait and we are human beings who need desperately to know how to wait if we are to achieve some of life's most abiding rewards.

Happiness in marriage comes to those who know how to wait. There was a time when young people were warned that if they married in haste they would repent in leisure. This is no longer true. We no longer repent in leisure. More and more young people are repenting in haste. They are too impatient to make the adjustments that marriage inevitably entails. They cannot wait to learn the tolerance that marriage always demands. They don't have the time to achieve the understanding which never comes quickly. They have not been taught that while love may come suddenly, happiness comes slowly.

Character comes to those who know how to wait. Goethe once revealed the truth in this matter when he said "Life is a quarry out of which we are to mold and chisel and complete a character." Notice all those time-consuming verbs. Character is distilled out of our daily confrontation with temptation, out of our regular response to the call of duty. It is formed as we learn to cherish principles and to submit to self-discipline. Character is the sum total of all the little decisions, the small deeds, the daily reactions to the choices that confront us. Character is not obtained instantly. We have to mold and hammer and forge ourselves into character. And that takes waiting.

Love for Judaism comes to those who know how to wait. Recently, when one of America's best known evangelists was attracting thousands to nightly gatherings, one of our people asked why we don't try these wholesale conversion tactics. Well, there are many reasons. But one of them is the fact that we don't have too much faith in spontaneous spiritual combustion. Like Jonah's gourd, that which comes in one day perishes in one day. A love of Judaism, an appreciation of the wealth of our heritage and its noble beauty have to be acquired slowly, painstakingly, in regular daily doses. "When thou walkest by the way, when thou liest down and when thou risest up." "Every day will I bless Thee and I shall praise Thy name for ever and ever." Judaism is a constant dimension of daily living; it is not a spectacular demonstration. Its symbol is the soft eternal light, not the dramatic firecracker. It requires steadiness and faithfulness and a great deal of waiting.

Education of the mind and heart requires waiting. The president of the United States has solicited the help of all who mold public opinion to address themselves to one of the crucial problems which confronts American youth today, the impatience which prompts so many of them to terminate their education with the completion of High School. These are the young people who will make very little contribution to the growth and development of our country, who will find themselves among the unemployables in an age which is progressively requiring more and more knowledge and training. Somehow these young people must be reached and persuaded that there is no short cut to a worthwhile career and there is no instant powdered form of education.

When James Garfield was the principal of Hiram College in Ohio, a father once came to him and asked whether the curriculum could not be simplified so that his son might be able "to go through by a shorter route." "Certainly," Garfield replied. "But it all depends upon what you want to make of your boy. When God wants to make an oak tree He takes a hundred years. When He wants to make a squash He requires only two months."

The Pilgrim Fathers made their way to America in the Mayflower whose average speed during much of the voyage across the Atlantic was two miles an hour. That same Atlantic will soon be

31

crossed by airplanes in two hours. But let us not be misled into believing that because physical journeys can be accelerated all of life's voyages can be speeded up. Life's most decisive adventures require patient and hopeful waiting. There is no instant happiness, there is no instant character, there is no instant love of Judaism, there is no instant development of the human being to his fullest potential. All of these things need huge quantities of waiting.

Having said all this, and I believe that it urgently needs saying and repeating, to a speed-addicted generation, we cannot stop at this point. We will not do justice to ourselves and to the imperative demands of our times unless we go on to say that there are indeed vital areas where waiting, far from constituting a virtue, becomes fatal to human aspirations and to progress. There are crucial domains both in our collective lives and in our personal lives where a saving *impatience* is called for, because we have already waited too long.

Consider in the first place the whole thorny problem of integration which may very well be the most decisive issue that confronts America not only internally but also in its aspiration to lead the free world in its march towards a more secure tomorrow.

In April of this year, eight Alabama clergymen made a public statement in which they described Martin Luther King's demonstration of protest against segregation in Birmingham, as "unwise and untimely." From a Birmingham jail King wrote a letter which ought to be required reading for every American. I should like to read a portion of that letter which bears directly upon our theme:

"Frankly, I have never yet engaged in a direct action movement that was 'well-timed,' according to the timetable of those who have not suffered unduly from the disease of segregation. For years now I have heard the word: 'Wait.' But when you have seen vicious mobs lynch your mothers and fathers at will and drown your sisters and brothers at whim; when you have seen hate-filled policemen curse, kick, brutalize, and even kill your black brothers and sisters with impunity; when you see the vast majority of your twenty million Negro brothers smothering in an airtight cage of poverty in the midst of an affluent society; when you suddenly find your tongue twisted and your speech stammering as you seek to explain to your six-year-old daughter why she can't go to the public amusement park that has just been advertised on television, and see tears welling up in her little eyes when she is told that Funtown is closed to colored children, and see the depressed clouds of inferiority begin to form in her little mental sky, and see her begin to distort her little personality by unconsciously developing a bitterness toward white people; when you have to concoct an answer for a five-year-old son asking in agonizing pathos: 'Daddy, why do white people treat colored people so mean?'; when you take a cross-country drive and find it necessary to sleep night after night in the uncomfortable corners of your automobile because no motel will accept you; when you are humiliated day in and day out by nagging signs reading 'white' men and 'colored'; when your first name becomes 'nigger' and your middle name becomes 'boy' (however old you are) and your last name becomes 'John,' and when your wife and mother are never given the respected title of 'Mrs.'; when you are harried by day and haunted by night by the fact that you are a Negro, living constantly at tiptoe stance, never quite knowing what to expect next, and plagued with inner fears and outer resentments; when you are forever fighting a degenerating sense of 'nobodiness'—then you will understand why we find it difficult to wait."

The pent-up frustration of the Negro is bursting out now with a fury which is greater for having been so long contained. Inevitably, there will be mistakes because we are not always at our wisest when we react to hurt. The specific demands of the Negro will have to be evaluated—each on its own merit. But there will be no purpose served in counselling the Negro any further to wait. He has already waited too long.

33

If the Negro has waited too long to be granted the freedom the white community has denied him, the Jew has also waited too painfully long for the justice the Christian world has too long withheld. I cannot describe the bitter disappointment I felt when the disclosure was made several months ago that the Ecumenical Council was urged to issue a statement condemning anti-Semitism but failed to do so for fear of antagonizing the Arab countries. How much longer must the Jew wait? Are not 6 million Jews long enough? When the Ecumenical Council reconvenes soon in Rome, I hope it will read carefully the words of the Executive Editor of the Catholic Star Herald, official organ of the Camden Diocese. Writing in that newspaper, the Rev. Msgr. Salvatore J. Adamo wrote last month: "There is an unfortunate element in our Catholic upbringing that conveys the idea that the Jews killed God." This, he said, leads Roman Catholics to "consider hatred toward the Jews not something sinful but rather a service to God. A clear pronouncement by the Vatican Council could help end this religious delusion once and for all." We have already waited much too long for such a pronouncement. No one should ask of us that we wait any longer.

I want to proceed now with our thought into another area which concerns us exclusively as Jews, where again we are waiting too long and where the waiting may be fatal to all that we cherish, to all for which this Synagogue stands and to which this day calls our renewed allegiance. We are waiting too long to find our way back to the Synagogue with anything like the regularity expected of us or the need for self-renewal which these difficult days create within us. While we wait our lives become progressively depleted of spiritual content. The estrangement between us and our heritage grows larger and more painful. While we wait, loyalties which should grow deeper begin to decay. Bonds which should be stronger begin to dissolve. Roots which should strike into the living soil of a vibrant faith rot away from lack of nourishment.

Our homes grow more barren. Our days suffer from a bleaching out of all Jewish color under the hot sun of tolerance and equality and comfort and abundance. We are waiting too long to become vitally involved in any program of Jewish observance, of Jewish study. While we wait the time for the harvest comes and we haven't even planted.

We are waiting too long as human beings to do what must be done today in a world which only gives us one day at a time without any assurance of tomorrow. Our days are so few, we frequently lament, and yet we procrastinate as though we had an endless supply.

We wait too long to show kindness. Edgar Fitzgerald, in a time of sadness, wrote to a friend, "Pray, do write to me. A few lines soon are better than a three-decker novel a month hence." How many lines are waiting for us to be written? How many words of solace need to be spoken?

We wait too long to be charitable. A magazine cartoon shows two old women draped in rags shivering over a meager fire. One asks, "What are you thinking about?" The other answers, "About the nice warm clothes the rich ladies will be giving us next summer." Too much of our giving is delayed until much of the need has passed for the recipient, and the joy of giving has been largely diminished.

A rich man once said to a friend, "Why is it everybody is always criticizing me for being miserly, when everyone knows I have made provision to leave everything I possess to charity when I die?"

"Well," said the friend, "let me tell you about the pig and the cow. The pig was lamenting to the cow one day about how unpopular he was. 'People are always talking about your gentleness and your kind eyes,' said the pig. 'Sure you give milk and cream, but I give even more. I give meat, I give bristles, and they even pickle my feet! Still nobody likes me. Why is this?'

35

"The cow thought a minute, and then said, 'Well, maybe it's because I give while I'm still living.' "

We wait too long to discipline ourselves and to take charge of our lives. We feed ourselves the vain delusions that it will be easier to uproot tomorrow the debasing habits we are permitting to tyrannize over us today and whose command over us grows more deeply entrenched each day they remain in power.

We wait too long to be parents to our children—when economic pressures will be fewer and other obligations less insistent —forgetting how brief is the time they are children, how swiftly life urges them on and away. We wait too long to speak the words of forgiveness that must be spoken, to set aside the hatreds that should be banished, to read the books that are waiting to be read, to see the beauty which is here to be seen, to hear the music which is here to be heard, to seek repentance which is within reach, to utter the prayers which are waiting to cross our lips, to perform the duties waiting to be discharged, to show the love that may no longer be needed tomorrow, to do in April what cannot be done in December. We wait too long in the wings when life has a part for us to play on the stage.

Some of the saddest words too frequently spoken at the end of a man's life go something like this: "He worked so hard all his life but never took the time to enjoy any pleasures. Now, when he could enjoy life, *nit da kein yoren,* he ran out of years." Whenever I hear this melancholy summary I always ask myself, Why, why did he postpone the enjoyment of life? Why did he wait? Is it possible to enjoy at 60 the pleasures that are available only at 40? Does financial security enable us to retrace our steps and to do now what should have been done then and could only have been done then? Is there any way of rewinding and replaying the film of life? There is no future joy which can compensate us for the legitimate joys we needlessly deny ourselves today. God, our prayer book reminds us, is waiting—waiting for us to stop waiting and to proceed with all haste to begin to do now, this day, all the things for which this day was made.

John Dryden has left us a few lines of poetry we would do well to listen to as the New Year dawns so that they might guide us to live our days without waiting for them to be gone before we find beauty in them:

"Happy the man, and happy he alone,
He who can call today his own;
He who, secure within, can say,
'Tomorrow, do thy worst; for I have lived today.

Be fair or foul, or rain or shine,
The joys I have possessed, in spite of fate, are mine.
Not heaven itself upon the past has power,
But what has been has been, and I have had my hour.' "

THE BEST YEARS OF OUR LIVES

Which are the best years of our lives? Childhood years? Years of youth? Middle age? The twilight years? Each stage is carefully weighed and the ultimate choice places opportunity in the hands of all.

Preached on Rosh Hashanah, 1948

4

The Best Years of Our Lives

THE RECURRENT refrain in the majestic liturgy of the High Holy Days is the prayer that the Divine Author will inscribe us in the Book of Life. A special urgency is conferred upon this prayer by the explicit reminders scattered throughout the Prayer Book that the years of our lives are few and fleeting.

Brief as life already is, we human beings tend to compress it even further by speaking, as we so often do, of "the best years of our lives." Thus we imply that not all of life is of equal worth. But let us pause today, when we pray for another year of life, to consider which years, if any, may properly be considered the best years of our lives.

Perhaps of all stages in life, the one most frequently singled out as constituting the best years is the childhood stage. Much popular sentiment is reflected in the Yiddish song, *Kinder Yorin, Ziese Kinder Yorin*—"Childhood Years, Sweet Childhood Years." How often do we look back nostalgically upon those tender grapes upon life's vine, happy carefree days, days marked by innocence and purity, free of anxiety and responsibility. Yes, we often say wistfully, those were the best years of our lives.

Our nostalgia for childhood is only an indication of how unreliable our memories often are. Distance in time, as in space, lends enchantment. We forget the heartaches of childhood, its pains, its loneliness, its fears and its struggles. We forget that to a child, his grief over a broken toy or a lost pet is as intense as the grief of an adult mourning the loss of a dear one or a fortune. A child lives in a world where the things he enjoys are usually

41

forbidden, while the things he is permitted he frequently doesn't enjoy. A child is irritated by parental restrictions and regimentation to which he sometimes passively submits while he dreams of running away from home. At other times his frustration finds violent expression in tantrums and torrents of tears. The same lack of understanding which prompts us to idealize the years of childhood also impels us often to inflict grievous wounds upon the sensitive heart of the child, wounds which the psychiatrist tells us may persist into adult life and cause serious emotional maladjustments. And most significantly, for every time we refer to childhood as "the good ol' days," our children say six times, "When I grow up." Perhaps when life's responsibilities weigh too heavily upon us we may be excused if we look back upon childhood through rose-colored glasses, but upon serious appraisal, childhood seems rather remote from "the best years of our lives."

Do the years of youth then constitute the best years of our lives? The De Leon Springs in Florida are a monument to the Spanish explorer who rather passionately thought so and died disappointed over his failure to locate the eternal youth-giving waters. His estimate of youth was shared by the writer who said: "If we realized at twenty what it means to be twenty, we would go mad from sheer joy." Youth has strength, vitality, imagination. It is a time of bold dreams and daring visions. It is a time of surplus energy and an unlimited capacity to believe. It is a time of courage and conviction. It is, in brief, a great time to be alive.

But here again, if we would extol the blessings of youth, we must not overlook its burdens. We must see youth through the eyes of young people, upon whom, as George Bernard Shaw lamented, youth is wasted. Youth has great power with little knowledge of how or where to apply it. Youth is capable of tremendous enthusiasm, but also of bitter disillusionment. And perhaps the greatest burden of youth is the awareness of vital decisions to be made without the necessary equipment to decide wisely. We usually think of youth as decided, determined, convinced. Actually, youth is searching, groping, perplexed. Youth outwardly appears like a sharp exclamation point. It is actually more of a question mark. Eugene O'Neill's play about youth was most aptly named, "Ah! Wilderness," for youth has no one well-defined goal, no single reliable signpost. It is drawn by conflicting goals, it is directed by contradictory signposts. No one who has not yet forgotten the bitter indecision of youth can too glibly call the years of youth "the best years of our lives."

We turn now to middle age and look there for the best years of our lives and here too there is much that can be said positively. In many significant areas, life does begin after forty. At that time our scale of values has been set. We have matured mentally. We are no longer uncertain in our chosen vocations or careers. We have mastered our occupations and have learned how to apply our energies most advantageously. Domestically too life begins to call for less strain and struggle. Our homes are established. If we have children, they are beginning to afford us the thrill of achievement and the pleasure of attainment. There are Bar Mitzvahs, graduations, marriages. Usually our children begin to repay the years of sacrifice and service we invested in their growth.

But if life begins after forty, it also begins to ebb at that time. Outwardly we begin to show aging symptoms and a look at ourselves in the mirror becomes progressively a greater test of our courage. Graying hairs and deepening lines begin to remind us of life's relentless forward movement. We begin to tire more quickly and we have to slacken our activity pace. New birthdays are greeted with diminishing enthusiasm and quickened apprehension. Inwardly we begin to show symptoms of boredom. With the disappearance of many of the problems that agitated us in our youthful years, life often tends to become somewhat too even, too regular, yes, monotonous. Life loses its originality and freshness.

In addition, by middle age we've become somewhat sadly convinced that our wild youthful dreams and ambitions are quite beyond our range and we'll have to do with much less than we envisioned for ourselves. We're not going to be the great professors, the great actors, the great industrialists, the great orators we couldn't help become at eighteen. We're just little people pretty much like millions everywhere. We understand what Thoreau meant when he wrote in his *Journal*: "The youth gets together his materials to build a bridge to the moon or perchance a palace or temple on the earth, and at length the middle-aged man concludes to build a woodshed with them."

Middle age, then, is not by any means a time of unmixed blessings.

Well, then we come to our last chronological category and look for the best years of our lives in old age. In the Jewish tradition particularly, old age is regarded with deep respect and reverence and the Bible even prescribes the courtesies and the honors due to the "hoary head." The poet Robert Browning caught the Jewish spirit quite accurately when he wrote in his poem "Rabbi Ben Ezra": "Come grow old along with me, the best is yet to be. The last of life for which the first was made." Yes, old age is "the last of life for which the first was made." Age usually mellows wisdom, nurses sorrows, bridles passions. It often brings peace to troubled spirits. At life's sunset the storms have spent their violence, greed and ambition have released their grip. And, in spite of the popular misconception to the contrary, old age is not without its creative powers. Oliver Wendell Holmes once said, "If you haven't cut your name on the door by the time you've reached forty, you might just as well put up your jack-knife." But the same Oliver Wendell Holmes didn't write *Over the Teacups* until he was seventy-five. Goethe completed *Faust* at eighty. Titian painted his historic masterpiece of the Battle of Lepanto at ninety-eight. Henrietta Szold's Hadassah work did not begin until she

44

was in her sixties, and Chaim Weizmann became the first President of Israel in his middle seventies.

Notwithstanding the blessings of old age and the fact that we all aspire to it, old age suffers from too many physical limitations to constitute the best years of our lives. Perhaps its most obvious and most serious burden is reflected in the High Holy Day prayer: "Cast us not off in old age, when our strength departs, forsake us not." The fear of being cast off and unwanted, the haunting dread of loneliness and being forsaken, these are the overwhelming fears of old age which rob it too often of the peace and serenity it could and should offer, and rule out old age as constituting the best years of our lives.

Well then, if neither childhood, nor youth, nor middle age, nor old age constitute the best years of our lives—are there then no best years in life? The answer paradoxically enough is that there are, and for each of us the best years of our lives are to be found in the present—right now. It matters not whether we are today celebrating our 25th Rosh Hashanah, our 45th or our 75th. Now, 5709, can be the best year of our life, for that is the only year we have at our disposal. 5708 is past and beyond recall. 5710 has not yet come. For some of us it may never come. But let us each make 5709 the best year of our lives. How can we do that?

The answer, I think, is reflected in the biblical summary of the life of mother Sarah. In reviewing her life, the Bible says, "And the life of Sarah was one hundred years, and twenty years and seven years." Now Hebrew is a language that loves brevity and the biblical style is usually terse and concise. But here we have a very obviously awkward way of saying that Sarah lived 127 years. Why the 100 years, the 20 years, the 7 years?

The Torah, it would seem, wanted to present more than a statistical summary of Sarah's life. It was also giving us a moral appraisal of her life. The Torah deliberately breaks down her total years into their component age levels—7, 20 and 100—to tell us

45

that Sarah's greatness lay in her ability to live each age level fully and properly. She enjoyed the respective blessings of each of life's successive stages and behaved in each stage as was proper and noble for that age level. She lived 7 with a song, 20 with a dream, 100 with a benediction. Unlike the modern writer who declared "Youth is a blunder; manhood a struggle; old age a regret," Sarah found the respective blessings in each of life's stages and enjoyed them; understood the responsibilities and fulfilled them. The best years of Sarah's life were, therefore, all her years. She had the wisdom to make them so.

It is this wisdom that we must cultivate. When a little girl puts on her mother's high-heeled shoes and wide-brimmed hat and unevenly smears some lipstick and rouge over her face, we laugh indulgently at the child's vain attempt to rush the years. It would be equally laughable, were it not so sad, if we could understand how often we ourselves, with no less futility, try to push back the years. The aging man who fancies himself a youthful Don Juan; the middle-aged woman who shops in the teen-age department and reads Seventeen; the wife who has never out-grown her infantile dependence and at the first squalls of marriage runs back to mother; the over-aggressive, ruthless businessman who has never left behind his childish sense of inferiority and inadequacy, and hence tries to demonstrate his great power while only betraying his lack of it for, as the saying has it, "Only the strong can be gentle"; the father who constantly seeks to avoid his parental obligations because emotionally he prefers to lean like the child rather than lift like the adult;—all these daily occurrences are evidence of our futile attempts to turn back the one-way clock of life, to paste on again the discarded pages of life's calendar. Psychologists call this the "regressive tendency" in human beings who, because they are children so long, never quite get over it. But, by whatever name it is called, it is simply our refusal or inability to mature, to cultivate in each of life's stages its respective

46

blessings and accept its responsibilities. By attempting to recapture past privileges which are irretrievably gone, we succeed only in losing those which are readily available. Like the dog in the fable who plunges into the water in an effort to snatch the bone from the mouth of the dog below, who in fact is merely his own reflection, and succeeds only in losing the bone which he does have, our vain yearning after our yesterdays only impoverishes our todays. What could be the best years of our lives become thereby pale, anaemic reflections without joy or delight. God grant us like Sarah to live 7 years, then 20 years, then 100 years.

But the biblical summary of Sarah's life contains one more vital clue to making the present the best year of our lives. Not only did Sarah succeed in enjoying the blessings and accepting the responsibilities of each age, but she also succeeded in carrying over into each succeeding age level some of the movable blessings of the previous one. Thus our sages say: "At 20 she preserved the wholesome beauty and charm of the 7 year old girl. At 100 she had still preserved the moral purity and integrity of the 20-year old girl." Note that our sages do not say that at 100 Sarah tried to retain the physical characteristics of the 20-year old girl. That would have been sheer folly. But she did retain some of the spiritual blessings which, while they are born in youth, need not die there.

Physicians of the body and mind are today in agreement that for healthy adult living, we must retain the child's capacity for play and recreation. For if all work and no play makes Jack a dull boy, it can make Jack's father many worse things than a dull man. It can make him high-strung, tense, irritable and generally not too fit to live with. From childhood we ought to try to carry over into mature life our thirst for more knowledge, our craving for new skills. There is a well-known engraving of the 16th century which represents an old man sitting in a child's wheel-chair with the Latin inscription over it, *Ancora Inporo*, "I still learn." This phrase was constantly on the lips of Michelangelo as in old age he carved marble and refused to rest. From youth we might try to preserve our faith in the future, our idealism, our boldness in facing life and our buoyant enthusiasm.

Perhaps it was this ability to carry into the advancing twilight the precious freightage accumulated during high noon that one kindly lady had in mind when a child asked her if she were old or young. "My dear," the elderly woman replied, "I have been young a very long time." At 100, she was still 20 and 7.

The present is life's holy ground. It is the hallowed meeting place of two eternities—the past and the future. If we try to live in either of those eternities we are courting emotional and physical disaster. And to our everlasting loss, we are also missing the abundant satisfactions so close at hand. It is in the present alone that we can and must live, in each "unforgiving minute" which comes laden with blessings beyond number.

It doesn't really take something exciting or spectacular or sensational to make this the best year of our lives. The exciting and the spectacular only enervate us momentarily and leave us later more painfully aware of life's humdrum existence. Daily happiness comes from the quiet, simple and normal satisfactions. Pleasant hours with our loved ones, moments lived in the presence of great spirits whose works we read or hear, a bit of study, a regular act of kindness, working for a communal cause, a few minutes of daily prayer. These are not by any means spectacular, but these are the things that really make life meaningful and satisfying. "Life," as Woodrow Wilson once correctly observed, "is not all running to a fire." And when Helen Keller was once asked what she would want to see most if she could have her eyesight restored for a moment, she answered: "The smile on a child's face and a sunset."

How fabulously wealthy you and I are!

"How strange it is," wrote Stephen Leacock, "the child says,

When I am a big boy. . . .' After marriage, the thought changes to 'When I'm able to retire.' And then when retirement comes, he looks back over the landscape traversed; a cold wind seems to sweep over it; somehow he has missed it all and it is gone. Life, we learn too late, is in the living, in the tissue of every day and hour."

No, my friends, it is not too late to learn this truth. As the year 5709 dawns, let us greet it with the salutation of the poet:

> Look to this day
> For it is life, the very life of life.
> For yesterday is but a dream
> And tomorrow is only a vision.
>
> But today, well lived, makes every yesterday a dream of
>   happiness
> And every tomorrow a vision of hope.
> Look well, therefore, to this day!
> Such is the salutation to the dawn.

And such, dear friends, is our salutation to the dawn of 5709, which I pray will be for each of us the very best year of our lives.

COVERING OUR SACKCLOTHS

The sackcloth, the symbolic garment of mourning, must sooner or later be worn by all. But one of the decisive differences between people is to be found in the way they wear the sackcloth. How indeed is it to be worn?

Preached on Yom Kippur, 1948
Reprinted from *Best Jewish Sermons of 5715-16*.

5

Covering Our Sackcloths

IT WAS A PERIOD of profound crisis for Samaria, the capital of the northern kingdom of ancient Israel. The King of Aram and his armies had besieged the city and its inhabitants were being starved to death. So intense had the hunger become, that mothers began to devour their young. When this news reached the King of Israel, the Bible tells us, "he rent his clothes . . . and the people looked and behold he had sackcloth within upon his flesh."

What a shock that sight must have been to the people! Each citizen knew of his personal troubles and tragedies. But how amazed they all must have been to see that beneath his royal robe, even the king was wearing a sackcloth—the symbol of personal sorrow and misfortune.

A deep truth speaks out to us from this incident—one that we ought to keep steadily before us especially in time of trouble. "Why did this happen to me?" people frequently ask the rabbi amidst sorrow, as though they alone were singled out by a malicious destiny as a target for its bitter shafts. We rarely stop to realize that even kings wear sackcloths.

The better I get to know people, the more impressed do I become with this one fact. Rare indeed is the individual without a sackcloth. Some of us wear the sackcloth of a deep frustration—a career to which we aspired but did not attain, a heart we sought but failed to win. Some of us wear the sackcloth of a haunting sense of inadequacy, or a deeply bruised conscience or an aching void left by the passing of a loved one. Blasted hopes, unrealized dreams, anguish and grief—is any life unfamiliar with them? Is not the sackcloth the common garment of all men?

There is a second significance to the biblical incident. The king wore his sackcloth *underneath*. He did not make of it his outer garment. He did not display it too prominently either to others or to himself. Here was an act of wisdom we would do well to emulate.

Fathers and mothers have sustained grievous losses during the past few years. Ours has been the tragic generation of which our sages spoke—the generation where parents bury children. Doubly tragic are those afflicted parents who have not learned to cover their sackcloths, who have made of it their outer garment.

In this matter, the rituals of Judaism concerning mourning contain an excellent prescription for emotional recovery from misfortune. Judaism prescribes a terminus to mourning. Just as it is a law that the *Kaddish* must be said for eleven months, so is it a law that the *Kaddish* may not be recited longer than eleven months. The *Shiva* period may likewise not be prolonged beyond seven days. After *Shiva*, the mourners must leave their sorrow-laden homes and go out into the healing sunshine of human society. After the prescribed period of mourning, the sackcloth must become an undergarment.

Some time ago, the widow of Colin Kelly was remarried. To some, her remarriage appeared as an act of disloyalty to the memory of her husband. In defense of what she had done, she said quite simply: "Of course you can never forget the past and the past will always color the present. But I do not think that you should let the past affect the present so much that there can be no future." This is an attitude which can usefully be applied to every sackcloth that life imposes. We must never let the past affect the present so much that there can be no future. If life is to be lived at all, we must learn to cover our sackcloths But with what shall we cover them?

The first thing we can use to cover our sackcloths, it seems to me, is the Robe of Understanding. We tend to regard trouble as an intruder and interloper who has no place in life's scheme of things. In the words of a popular song, we often think that the world was made only for fun and frolic. Nothing makes the wearing of life's sackcloths more difficult to endure, than the fact that we are not prepared for them.

If we would learn to wear life's sackcloths properly we must cover them with the Robe of Understanding. We must realize that, as the Bible puts it, "Man is born to trouble." Trouble far from being a gate-crasher in life's arena actually has a reserved seat there. Human life is attended at its beginning by the piercing cries of the infant and at its end by the agonized wailing of the bereaved. In between, there are sadness, heartbreak, disease. For that reason, the great tragedians of literature have not wanted for themes. All they had to do was to observe life carefully and report it faithfully and the tragedy spelled itself out. "Man is born to trouble."

I know that many will feel that such a gloomy view of life leads to pessimism and despair. Actually, the reverse is true. If we accept realistically life's sombre back-drop then the manifold blessings we enjoy will emerge in bolder relief. The love which nourishes us, the friendship which warms us, the beauty which inspires us, the health which sustains us—all these and the countless other blessings which are ours will be all the more gratefully welcomed.

God grant us the Robe of Understanding to cover our sackcloths.

But the Robe of Understanding, beautiful and becoming as it is, is not enough. For at best it can only teach us the spirit of resignation to our troubles, and it is not enough to merely accept trouble. We must do more. We must learn to use trouble and convert it into a stepping stone to triumph. For that we need the Robe of Wisdom.

In the 48th chapter of the Book of Isaiah, there is a very re-

55

markable verse. The prophet is chastizing his people and among other things he says to them, according to Moffat's translation: "I purged you, but nothing came of it, testing you in the furnace but all in vain." Here the prophet is rebuking his people for having been through the furnace of affliction and having learned nothing from the experience, "What," he is asking them, "have you to show for all the sufferings you experienced? The tragedy is not that you endured pain; the tragedy is that your pain was wasted, leaving you none the wiser, none the better."

Yes, the prophet expected his people to do more than accept trouble. He expected them to use it. The fact is that some of life's most valuable lessons can be and have been learned precisely in the classroom of adversity. We discern most clearly many a basic truth of life when our eyes are dimmed by tears. Robert Browning Hamilton expressed a common human reaction when he wrote:

"I walked a mile with Pleasure
She chattered all the way
But left me none the wiser
For all she had to say.

"I walked a mile with Sorrow
And ne'er a word said she
But oh the things I learned from her
When Sorrow walked with me."

We speak very often of "victims of circumstance"—people whose souls are crushed beneath the wheels of unfortunate events. We would do well to start thinking of "victors of circumstance" —people who use even negative circumstance and distill from it some new insight into life, keener understanding or more beautiful character. We often speak of people who were successful because they knew how to take advantage of good "breaks." We would do well to start thinking that people can be successful if they have the wisdom to capitalize on their bad "breaks." It is possible to be like Wordsworth's "Happy Warrior."

> "Who doomed to go in company with Pain
> And Fear, and Bloodshed, miserable train!
> Turns his necessity to glorious gain."

Or as the Psalmist puts it:

> "They pass through a valley of tears and
> convert it into a life-giving fountain."

God grant us the Robe of Wisdom to cover our sackcloths.

Thirdly, may I suggest that we cover our sackcloths with the Robe of Service. There is a legend of a sorrowing woman who came to a wise man with the heart-rending plea that he return to her, her only son whom she had just lost. He told her that he could comply with her request on one condition. She would have to bring to him a mustard seed taken from a home entirely free from sorrow. The woman set out on her quest. Years elapsed and she did not return. One day the wise man chanced upon her, but he hardly recognized her, for now she looked so radiant. He greeted her and then asked her why she never kept their appointment. "Oh" she said in a tone of voice indicating that she had completely forgotten about it, "Well this is what happened. In search of the mustard seed, I came into homes so burdened with sorrow and trouble that I just could not walk out. Who better than I could understand how heavy was the burden they bore? Who better than I could offer them the sympathy they needed? So I stayed on in each home as long as I could be of service. And," she added apologetically, "please do not be angry, but I never again thought about our appointment."

Here is a most profound truth to remember when life makes us don a sackcloth. Trouble and sorrow naturally make us think only of ourselves. But after the first impact of the blow has worn off, our emotional recovery depends upon our ability to forget ourselves. And there is no better way of forgetting about ourselves than by thinking of and serving others. Human experience every day confirms the truth of the legend. He who can do no better after sorrow than engage in the futile search for the mustard seed to restore the loss which is in fact irretrievable, is destined to spend years of avoidable heartache. But happy is he who can rise from his mourner's bench and so lose himself in the service of others that he finds himself unknowingly climbing the mountain of healing to which the road of service inevitably leads.

God grant us the Robe of Service to cover our sackcloths.

The last and most significant robe with which we might cover our sackcloths is the Robe of Faith—faith in the immortality of the souls of our beloved.

The *Yizkor* prayer which is recited four times every year makes a bold affirmation about the human soul. It declares that death has no dominion over it. "May God remember the soul of my mother. . . ." "May God remember the soul of my son. . . ." The soul survives to be remembered. It does not perish with the death of the body. This same faith is echoed in the *El Mole Rahamim* prayer where we speak of the soul as being bound up in "the bond of life everlasting." Thus Judaism, like all great religions, teaches that "Death is not a period which brings the sentence of life to a full stop. It is only a comma that punctuates it to loftier existence." Here is the most comforting of all robes to cover the sackcloth of bereavement.

To be sure, like all daring affirmations of Judaism, the belief in immortality cannot be scientifically demonstrated. It is as the philosopher Santayana correctly called it "the Soul's invincible surmise." But if it is a "surmise" it is one of mankind's most persistent surmises. From ancient man in his primitive beliefs down through the long corridors of time stretching into the present most sophisticated faiths, men have always held the human soul

58

indestructible. Nor has this belief been limited to religious thinkers alone. Philosophers, poets, physicians, scientists, all answer
"present" when the roll is called among the believers that death
is not the end. How the soul survives is, of course, a mystery. It
is no less a mystery, however, than how the soul arrives. It origi-
nates with the Source of all Life and flows back to its origin.

When death robs us of a loved one the pain of parting can be
assuaged through our faith that the essence of our beloved lives
on not only in our hearts and in our memories but more especially
with the Author of life Himself. It is this faith which burst forth
out of Emerson after the passing of his little son. "What is
excellent," he wrote in his "Threnody," "as God lives, is permanent."

God grant us the Robe of Faith to cover our sackcloths.

The story of a king introduced our problem. The story of
another monarch will sum up our solution. Alexander the Great,
it is told, once commissioned an artist to paint his portrait. He
gave him only two conditions. It was to be an exact likeness, un-
falsified. Moreover, it was to be handsome and attractive. The
artist had no easy task, for over his right eye, Alexander had a
prominent battle scar. The artist was thus confronted with a painful dilemma. To omit the scar would be a violation of the first
condition. To include it would be a violation of the second.
Finally, the artist came up with the solution. He painted Alexander
in a pensive mood, his face supported by his right hand with his
forefinger covering the scar.

We cannot eliminate life's scars upon our souls for we should
not be true to life. Nor can we permit them to be prominently
viewed, for they would then make life ugly and unlivable.

We must learn to cover the scars upon our souls, the sackcloths
upon our flesh. With the Robe of Understanding which teaches
us to accept trouble as part of the price we pay for being human;
with the Robe of Wisdom which helps us use trouble, and con-

vert it into triumph; with the Robe of Service which enables us
to recover our own strength while at the same time bringing
strength to others; with the Robe of Faith which whispers comforting assurance that the soul is mightier than death; with these
robes, let us cover our sackcloths and thus make the portrait of
our lives beautiful and inspiring to behold.

DISTURBING THE COMFORTABLE

In an age where tens of millions are spent annually to tranqui-
lize us, the Shofar's message is like a shrill alarm clock. To
what should we awaken? The words of Maimonides point to a
challenging answer.

Preached on Rosh Hashanah, 1957
Reprinted in Best Jewish Sermons of 5717-18.

6

Disturbing the Comfortable

RELIGION, it has been pointed out, has two almost contradictory functions to perform in our lives. On the one hand, it should comfort us when we are disturbed. On the other, it should disturb us when we are comfortable.

Any student of Jewish history knows how supremely well Judaism performed its first function. Were it not for the life-restoring reservoirs of strength and hope that the Jew constantly tapped in his heritage he could not possibly have survived the repeated efforts to destroy him.

Heinrich Heine was not rhapsodizing when he called our Bible, the medicine chest of humanity. For all of life's bruises and aches, for the soul's distress and anguish, for our grief and loneliness, for our disillusionment and despair, the Bible contains most effective healing balm. It can comfort the disturbed as no other book can.

But when we have said all this, we have not exhausted the role of the Bible in our history. The Bible has also been called with some justification the most anti-Semitic book ever written. The prophets were unrelenting and outspoken in cataloguing their people's sins and denouncing their transgressions. Open almost any page of the prophets and you are likely to read something like this:

"How is the faithful city become a harlot,
She that was full of justice,
Righteousness lodged in her
But now murderers.
Thy silver is become dross,

63

Thy wine mixed with water,
Thy princes are rebellious,
And companions of thieves.
Every one loves bribes
They judge not the fatherless
Neither does the cause of the widow come to them."

The prophets who could soothe with motherly compassion could scold with bitterest condemnation. The same prophet Isaiah who comforted the disturbed with "Comfort ye, comfort ye my people" could disturb the comfortable with, "Woe unto them who are at ease on Zion."

What shall be the message of this day? Shall we comfort or disturb?

I will confess to you that in thinking of this day's message I was perplexed as I have rarely been by this very question. How well I know the anxieties that gnaw at our hearts. In the congregation this morning are those upon whom sorrow has recently laid its heavy hand, those whose hearts are seared by guilt, those who have lost their way and those who have not yet found it, the lonely and the betrayed, the misled and the tempted, the bored and the frightened, the agitated and the restless, the handicapped and the haunted, all are here today. How many disturbed cry out for comfort! How tempting to try to address oneself to these all too human and all too prevalent predicaments.

And yet, I could not help but be aware that this aspect of religion has already received so much emphasis as to threaten to reduce religion to a spiritual tranquilizer. The magic word in so many messages written by clergymen these days is "relax."

"You Must Relax."

"The Art of Relaxation."

"Relax For Easy Power."

"Relax and Live."

All wisdom of religion is being compressed into the blessed word "relax," like abbreviating an 88 note piano into one note.

I sometimes have the feeling that this distortion of the character of religion is inspired to some degree by the desire of the clergymen to compete with the drug-stores and the very lucrative business they are doing these days selling tranquilizers. It is estimated that last year some 35 million prescriptions were filled for tranquilizers, representing a cost of 150 million dollars!

I don't presume to be able to evaluate the effectiveness and the worth of these "happiness" pills. From what I can gather, it would seem that in the medical profession itself there is divided opinion as to their value and even their safety. What is significant about them however, is that they reveal a widespread desire among millions of us to be rid of tension and anxiety.

"What is it that we are trying to run away from?" asks a writer in a recent article. And he answers: "From normalcy, that's what! From stresses and strains that the human animal was designed to stand and is perfectly capable of standing."

He goes on to say: "Consider some of the uses one manufacturer recommends that his tranquilizer be taken for:

Financial worries.

Family tensions caused by sickness, weddings, funerals.

Troubles stemming from differences of opinion.

Apprehensions connected with approaching parenthood.

Tension in children resulting from the arrival of a new baby or a move to a new home.

Tension among adolescents caused by social competition, increased responsibility, first jobs.

The list might be funny if it were not frightening. All these crises are the normal problems of living."

To be rid of them means to stop being human beings and become vegetables. To preach the gospel of relaxation to the exclusion of all else seems to stamp one as an accomplice in this dehumanizing process.

So it would seem that this matter of comforting the disturbed has already been carried too far.

While this problem was still agitating me, I chanced upon a very perceptive article by Norman Cousins in the *Saturday Review* entitled, "Checklist of Enemies." In it he points out how each of us in his own way can betray democracy: the common man, the government official, the scientist. Then he said something which I underscored in red because he seemed to be talking directly to me:

"The enemy is any man in the pulpit . . . who is a dispenser of balm rather than an awakener of conscience. He is pre-occupied with the need to provide personal peace of mind rather than to create a blazing sense of restlessness to set things right."

As I read these words they rang the bell of memory. This challenge I recognized at once as the central theme of Rosh Hashanah, the very core of its meaning. For what does the Shofar represent, if not a call to awakening? We remember how Maimonides explained it: It calls out to us, he said, "Awake ye sleepers from your slumber and rouse yourselves from your lethargy."

The Shofar is not a soothing voice chloroforming us into a sense of well-being, but a shrill piercing call stimulating us to redress the world's wrongs. It is not a lullaby but an alarm clock. It does not whisper "relax." It cries out "awake." It does not encourage complacency. It shatters it. It asks us to become alert human beings who care desperately, whose life has a sense of deadline and intensity.

To raise relaxation to a philosophy of life is like relaxing the mainspring of a watch. What is left may be very handsome but it is quite worthless. A relaxed watch does not strike the hours. When the tension goes out of our lives we have lost our most distinguishing human characteristic. Animals as far as we know do not feel tension. Cows remain contented as long as they keep chewing.

What we should strive for, it would seem then, is not the elimination of tension, but the careful selection of our tensions. So many of our tensions are simply unworthy of us.

All too often, "too many necessities are the mother of tension." We delude ourselves and sometimes destroy ourselves because we think that happiness resides in things. We forget that contentment is achieved not by adding to our possessions but by curbing our desires.

Another frequent source of tension comes from exaggerating petty annoyances and irritations. Ulcers, someone has said with much truth, come from mountain climbing over molehills.

And who can estimate the needless tensions we suffer from anticipating troubles that never strike? Emerson spoke to many of us when he said:

> "Some of your hurts you have cured
> And the sharpest you still have survived
> But what torments of grief you endured
> From evils that never arrived."

Maimonides who interprets the blasts of the Shofar as a spiritual reveille, as a call to awakening, goes on to indicate the areas of life worthy of our tensions, of our caring. He indicates the three things about which we should each of us be disturbed. Let us consider each briefly.

In the first place, he asks us to feel the tension between what we are and what we are capable of becoming. "Remember your Creator," is the way he puts it. What does it mean to remember our Creator? It means many things but certainly one of the most apparent implications is that we are creatures of the Divine, we have a noble descent, a lofty pedigree. "Beloved is man," taught

67

Rabbi Akiba, "for he was created in the Divine Image. But God's love for him took on an added dimension when man awoke to the truth that he was created in the Divine Image."

This awareness that there is a spark of divinity in each of us means not only that every human life is infinitely precious but also that it possesses unlimited potentialities. We are indeed, as the Psalmist exclaimed in rapture, only little lower than the angels.

But do our lives always reflect this grandeur? Are we as generous as we might be? Are we as humble as we ought to be? Are we as forgiving, as understanding, as tolerant as we could be? How often during the past year have we betrayed our conscience, forfeited our human birthright, sacrificed principle on the altar of pleasure or profit? Who can count the times when the clamor of our own petulant desires made us deaf to the pleas of the sick, the heavy-hearted, the outraged? On how many occasions have we permitted anger and prejudice to blind our judgment? How frequently did we put selfishness above duty and expediency above morality? How often did we answer the call of the wild and turn a deaf ear to the pleading of the angels within? Is there one among us who can honestly reflect on these things and not feel the powerful tension between the mire to which we so often descend and the pull of the stars which beckon us heavenward? Who is exempt from being disturbed over the intolerable tug of war within us between life's downward drag and our soul's upward reach?

This is a day for feeling tense not tranquil, for feeling disturbed not comfortable. Awake ye sleepers from your slumber, says the Shofar. "Remember your Creator," says Maimonides.

There is a second tension Maimonides would have us feel— the tension between what we habitually do and what we are capable of doing, between the mundane character of our lives and the holy adventures they might become.

"Ye who forget eternal truths in the trifles of the hour," is Maimonides accusation against us. That's a striking way of putting one of our most widespread failings—bypassing eternal truths for momentary trifles, trying so desperately to be up to date that we forget to devote ourselves to the timeless, striving so hard to achieve the things which perish that we forget to give a portion of ourselves to the things that will live forever, straining for the means of living and overlooking the ends for which we should live, giving high priority to life's diversions and only marginal moments to its crucial purposes.

What one mother recently said of her teen age daughter fits many of us uncomfortably well. "She's a good girl," her mother said "but she is constantly majoring in the minors." Majoring in the minors—that's what makes so much of our life trivial and inconsequential. I haven't yet read the book, but what a commentary is the title on the hollowness of contemporary American life. *Where did you go? Out. What did you do? Nothing.* With more leisure than any society ever enjoyed, and with a thousand worthy causes pleading for our energies one of America's major problems today is boredom. One physician claims that boredom actually kills people. Being "bored to death," is not simply a figure of speech. That, I take it, comes largely from majoring in the minors.

I wish that we would each use time stubs the way we use check stubs so that at the end of the year we could take inventory and see how we spent the hours of each day. The accounting would prove quite humbling I'm afraid. How many of us would be proven spendthrifts of life's most precious currency—Time.

As we compare our normal preoccupations with our potential pursuits we have good reason for being disturbed.

Awake ye sleepers from your slumbers, says the Shofar. "Remember the eternal truths," pleads Maimonides.

Lastly, Maimonides would have us feel the tension between

the Jewishness of our lives as they are and what, with some self-discipline, they might become.

"Look well into your souls," he pleads.

It is common knowledge that in recent years a silent revolution of impressive dimensions has taken place within the American Jewish community. The flight from Judaism has been arrested and to an appreciable extent the process has been reversed. Parents who had consciously discarded much of their spiritual and cultural baggage in an effort to facilitate their exodus from Jewish life have lived to see their children return to rebuild the ramparts they had forsaken. The amazing mushrooming of imposing synagogues, the constantly expanding enrollment in religious schools, the flourishing memberships in a host of fraternal, philanthropic, cultural and Zionist-oriented organizations, these are only the most conspicuous indications that we are witnessing a phenomenon undreamed of, or perhaps only dreamed of, a short generation ago. This dramatic turn of events has prompted one keen observer to remark that what the children of Jewish immigrants to America wished to forget, their grandchildren wish to remember.

Despite this heartening development, all is far from well in the household of American Israel. Too often, the reaffirmation of the Jewish identity has been accompanied by only the most nebulous understanding of the nature of that identity. What does it mean to be a Jew? What is the character of the heritage which is ours? What duties does it spell out? What blessings does it offer? Why persist in perpetuating for ourselves and our children this Jewish label which bigots and madmen periodically convert into a target? These crucial questions have not been asked with the earnestness and the insistence they warrant. Small wonder and a great pity that we are too often innocent of the answers, that too many of us regard our Jewishness as an inescapable fate rather than a priceless privilege. A modern Jewish philosopher delivered an indictment which contains a disquieting amount of truth when he said: "Judaism is rich, but the individual Jew is a beggar."

The nervous times during which we live confer special urgency upon our need to rediscover our heritage and to relate ourselves to it with a sense of personal involvement. Ours are indeed dangerous days. The threat of total annihilation hovers above us. Within ourselves there is mounting evidence of lost moorings and uncertain anchorage. There is a growing recognition that if we are to avoid the threatened atomization of man and his world, we will have to muster a spiritual power greater than the destructive forces we have unleashed. Where else will we find that power if we seek it not in our ancestral legacy?

Ours is a tradition ripe with the wisdom of years and strengthened by a thousand anvils. Judaism was a venerable faith before other powerful religions were born. For it, millions were innocently martyred. By it, millions more have nobly and compassionately lived. Despite its antiquity, it shows none of the infirmities of age. It remains throbbing and dynamic, capable of clothing us with dignity and hallowing our lives with high purpose. If we would strive to possess that which we rightfully own, we would come into an abundant inheritance which our fathers painstakingly stored up for us to enjoy. We would then exclaim in the words of Tennyson:

> We are the Ancients of the earth
> And in the morning of the times.

But that feeling will come to us only if we begin to look upon Judaism in terms of commitment, in terms of *mitzvot*, in terms of daily duties, to study and observe, to bring Judaism into our homes and into our lives.

"Awake ye sleepers from your slumbers" says the Shofar. "Look well into your souls," counsels Maimonides.

71

This then is the message of this day for our day. It is meant to arouse us, to sensitize us so that we feel life's saving tensions—between what we are and what we, as children of God, can become, between what we habitually do and what we should be doing, between the Jewish lives we are leading and the Jewish lives we could be living.

The blast of the Shofar is designed not to reassure us that all is well with us but to call attention to the many areas which need mending; not to pamper us but to challenge us; not to feed us spiritual tranquilizers but to sound a moral alert.

Some time ago, a sheep-herder in the hills of Idaho sent a letter to one of the national radio programs in which he made a strange request. He explained that he listened to the program every week and that the radio was his sole companion in his lonely occupation. His old violin which he used to play was now so badly out of tune as to be worthless. "I wonder if you would be kind enough" he went on "to pause on your 10 o'clock program on Tuesday morning to strike an "A" so that I might tune my violin and enjoy its music again."

The shepherd's request was honored. On the 10 o'clock program the following Tuesday, the announcer read his unusual request to his nationwide audience and then an "A" was sounded so that the shepherd might tune his violin and play it again.

On Rosh Hashanah God bids us to sound an "A" on the Shofar so that each of us might tune up the instruments of our lives and proceed to play beautiful music.

Heavenly Father Who dwells also in our heart,
Comforter of the disturbed and disturber of the comfortable,
Heal our infirmities, shatter our indifference.

On this day of sounding the Shofar,
May we heed well its call to awake from our moral slumbers
and to rouse overselves from our spiritual lethargy.

DISTURBING THE COMFORTABLE

May it remind us of our noble descent
and the heights we can attain.
May it stimulate us to devote our lives to
high purposes and noble pursuits.

May it inspire us, as faithful sons
and daughters of Israel,
to know our heritage
and to live by it.

Thus may we be inscribed in the book of creative
and noble life.

FINDING OURSELVES

A wise inscription on a bench beside a quiet pool of water calls attention to one of our perils and one of our needs. As Americans, as Jews, as men and women, we should read carefully and reflect earnestly on what that inscription says to us.

Preached on Rosh Hashanah, 1960

7

Finding Ourselves

IN LAKE WALES, FLORIDA, by the Bok Singing Tower there is a bench beside a quiet pool of water. On the back of that bench there is this inscription: "I come here to find myself. It is so easy to get lost in the world."

Today I want to talk about these two simple sentences. Let us treat the second sentence first because it calls attention to our problem, the danger of getting lost in the world. This problem has many ramifications. In the opinion of some of our most respected thinkers and writers, this happens to be the foremost problem confronting America as a nation today.

A few months ago, the *New York Times* in conjunction with *Life* Magazine ran a series of articles on the subject of National Purpose. These articles have just appeared in book form. The eminent men who contributed to the series seemed to share the conviction that America, for all its unprecedented and unrivaled wealth, has lost something vital—a something which could be fatal to its future and to the whole free world. Archibald MacLeish, one of the participants in the discussion, put the problem in bold perspective when he wrote: "We are prosperous, lively, successful, inventive, diligent . . . but, nevertheless and notwithstanding, something is wrong and we know it.

"The trouble seems to be that we don't feel right with ourselves or with the country. It isn't only the Russians. We have outgrown the adolescent time when everything that was wrong with America was the fault of the Russians and all we needed to do to be saved was to close the State Department and keep the

Communists out of motion pictures. It isn't just the Russians now; it's ourselves. It's the way we feel about ourselves as Americans. We feel that we've lost our way in the woods, that we don't know where we are going . . . if anywhere."

So, here we have it. Here is the diagnosis of our national malady. America has gotten lost in the world.

When we move from the American scene to the Jewish scene, the problem is no less acute. For us American Jews, it is so easy to get lost in the world.

Not very long ago, our major problem in America was that Jews did not want to perpetuate their identity. Judaism was associated with the old world. It was something foreign, something to be shed and discarded. There was abroad a conscious and deliberate process of assimilation. Many of our people felt that they would solve the Jewish problem by dissolving the Jew. In short, they wanted to get lost in the world.

Then there came the Nazi holocaust which underscored the futility of escape as a solution. In quick order there followed the disenchantment with communism which was revealed in all its moral and spiritual nakedness. Jewish loyalties, long dormant, were quickened by the rebirth of Israel. Here in America, the end of World War II was marked by a growing religious consciousness. All of these had their very profound impact on the Jew. Together, they served to reverse the trend away from Jewish life and brought back to the fold many who had been on their way out. Jewish life in America has flourished mightily in the last two decades. Synagogues, Jewish schools, Jewish organizations are alive with numerous activities, programs. For all these outward signs of robust good health, for all our affirmation of our Jewishness and our desire to perpetuate it, students of the Jewish scene are deeply apprehensive about our spiritual future in this land of freedom. The Jewish press has recently been debating the moot question: "Does American Jewry Have a Future?" Why are they questioning whether

78

our past has a future, whether we ourselves have a future here as Jews? Because observation has taught them that it is possible to build synagogues and stay away from them, to pay lip service to a tradition and disregard it, to extol a heritage and remain unfamiliar with it.

Earnest observers are questioning our future as Jews because they see beneath the surface a dilution of the contents of Jewish life, a slow but steady process of attrition eating away at the vitals of Jewish life; hallowed observances being discarded; Jewish homes emptied of any distinctive Jewish content, or symbols or sounds or rituals; Jewish lives losing all uniqueness.

Because the process is gradual and largely involuntary, because the inner corrosion is taking place under the cover of outward feverish activity, we are prone to develop a false sense of security. The sober truth however is that for the American Jew it is so easy to get lost in the world.

The problem of getting lost in the world is one which not only confronts us as Americans, and as Jews, but also as human beings. It is so frightfully easy to get lost in the world. Life, like a careless laundryman, has a nasty way of shrinking our ideals and our hopes, bleaching the color out of our principles and our values.

We come into maturity carrying the banner of youthful enthusiasm and noble goals only to suffer what the poet Shelley called "the contagion of the world's slow stain." W. Somerset Maugham made this point sharply in one of his stories entitled "The Colonel's Lady." The wife of a rather self-satisfied English Colonel suddenly achieves fame by writing a book in which she tells of her tragic loss of a great love. This exposes her husband to ridicule among their friends and he angrily confronts his wife with the demand that she tell him who was that secret lover of whom she writes so tenderly. At first she refuses but when the Colonel persists and even threatens her with violence, she breaks down and confesses: "You were that lover! You—when we first married—when you were a wonderful, noble, idealistic young man, filled with lofty principles and noble visions—the man with whom I fell in love. But that young man died long ago. All I have left now is you as you have become—a successful man as the world measures it, but a man without any integrity or decency, a man for whom I have lost all respect—a man whom I can no longer really love."

We feel for the wife; we suffer with the Colonel. He has achieved success but he has gotten lost in the world. He has been infected by "the contagion of the world's slow stain."

Who among us has been innoculated against this contagion? Who can hear this story without drawing some painful personal parallels?

> Across the fields of yesterday
> He sometimes comes to me
> A little lad just back from play
> The lad I used to be.
>
> And yet he smiles so wistfully
> Once he has crept within
> I wonder if he hopes to see
> The man I might have been.
>
> (*Thomas S. Jones, Jr.*)

There is no simple or single explanation why we get lost in the world. But surely one of the most persuasive reasons in our time is the addiction to the worship of success, the insatiable hunger for things, the soul-consuming preoccupation with status. These things combine to blur our vision. They throw our sense of values out of focus. They tempt us to blink at the truth of an old proverb which teaches that he who sacrifices his conscience to ambition burns the picture to obtain the ashes. They cause us to confuse a man's worth with his wealth, his stature with his status. We forget that what a man is, is of infinitely more significance than what a man has.

In the bleak and dreary winter of 1929, there gathered around a conference table in Chicago's Edgewater Beach Hotel nine men who were beyond question the world's most successful industrialists of the time. The fortunes of at least one-half of the world's population hung upon their decisions. By every popular standard, they had to be counted among the giants of the earth. The nine men were: Charles Schwab, the president of the world's largest steel empire; Samuel Insull, the president of the world's largest public utilities combine; Howard Hopson, the president of the world's largest gas company; Arthur Cutten, the world's most powerful wheat speculator; Jesse Livermore, the biggest bear in Wall Street; Ivar Kreuger, the director of the world's largest monopoly; Albert Fall, a member of the Cabinet of the United States; Richard Whitney, the president of the New York Stock Exchange; Leon Fraser, the president of the Bank of International Settlements.

Twenty-five years later Charles Schwab was dead, a bankrupt. Samuel Insull was a penniless fugitive from justice. Howard Hopson was insane. Arthur Cutten died insolvent abroad. Jesse Livermore was a suicide. Ivar Kreuger was a suicide. Albert Fall was released from prison that he might die at home. Richard Whitney had just completed a term at Sing Sing. Leon Fraser was a suicide.

It is so easy to get lost in the world! And because it is, we Jews on Rosh Hashanah, come here, to the synagogue, to find ourselves. For us, the synagogue pew is our bench by the quiet pool. For the quiet pool we substitute the life-giving waters of our Torah and our tradition. And if we are to find ourselves, we must look at that which is greater than ourselves, toward God Himself. This is the true significance of our prayer: "Remember

81

us to life O King who desirest life and inscribe us in the book of Life, a life lived for Thy sake."

We find ourselves when we discover that we are children of God, who gave us life as a trust, to be lived in a way worthy of Him who entrusted it to our care. On this day of judgment we submit our lives to the judgment of God.

For America to find herself, she must rediscover the true sources of her power and her greatness. President Eisenhower has appointed a Commission on National Goals to issue "a call to greatness" to the American nation. I hope that the Commission will remind us that the greatness of America is not in its missiles, or submarines or nuclear weapons. America's greatness does not lie in the number of its two-car families, its TV sets, its miles of superhighways. Our weapons are, of course, indispensable for survival. Our machines and appliances make life more comfortable. But the essence of America's greatness lies in the greatness of her ideals, her passionate belief in the equality of all men, the sacredness of each man. America's greatness lies in her extraordinary capacity to share her extravagant bounty with the hungry of the earth, the poor, the naked, the homeless. America's greatness lies in her ability to champion the cause of morality and justice both at home and abroad without considering the cost, because in its finest moments America has known the truth of our Bible: "Righteousness exalts a nation but sin is a reproach to any people."

And perhaps the most crucial test of America's greatness will lie in her ability to inspire in the hearts of her sons and daughters the same enthusiasm for democracy, the same passion to preach it and sacrifice it as Russia has been able to elicit on behalf of the false god of communism.

In this critical juncture in world history, even more than in Walt Whitman's day, is it true of America:

Humanity with all its fears
With all its hopes of future years
Is hanging breathless on thy fate.

This is the essence of our national purpose. This is how America can remain true to her pledge of being a nation "under God." This is how America will once again find herself.

If we American Jews are not to get lost in the world, we will each have to take our Judaism seriously. Casual Jews too often become Jewish casualties. Taking Judaism seriously involves more than financial responsibility to the synagogue. It is not only a question of giving. It is also a matter of taking, taking what is rightfully ours, what a hundred generations of Jews have accumulated for us to enjoy.

It means enjoying the rest and the liberation from enslavement to the world which the Shabbat offers weekly.

It means enriching our homes with the poetry and pageantry of Jewish observance, the beauty of Jewish ritual, the music of Jewish song.

It means anchoring our lives against the storms of fortune with the faith of the Psalmist: "The Lord is my light and my salvation; whom shall I fear? The Lord is the fortress of my life; of whom shall I be afraid?"

Taking Judaism seriously means engaging in the most uniquely Jewish discipline—the study of Torah.

I am exceedingly proud to be able to announce that the Board of Directors of our congregation has passed a resolution committing every member of the Board to participate in a program of Jewish study. Henceforth, no one will be eligible for election to our Board without a prior signed commitment to engage in some form of Jewish education. This commitment is added to the one adopted several years ago which makes it mandatory for Board members to attend services regularly. By its most recent action, our Board helps to put the accent in Jewish life where it belongs—on personal growth and development as Jews. I call upon each of us to follow the sublime example our lay leaders have set for us. We have come here today to find ourselves as Jews. Let us resolve to make sure by our personal commitments and actions throughout the year that we shall not get lost in the world.

Lastly, we have come as human beings who are so easily diverted from the highroad of life into its alleys and backyards.

Temptation, false values, loss of confidence, lack of courage— these are only some of the pitfalls. Pettiness, selfishness, fear—are others.

No one has the right to say to another fellow adventurer: Brother, you have lost the way. But each of us has an obligation to ask ourselves—Have I lost the way? Have I turned my back on what I know to be true and just? Have I betrayed my own finest instincts? Have I misused God's gifts of body and mind?

This is what we mean when we say that Rosh Hashanah is a day for *heshbon hanefesh*—taking inventory into our lives. It is an occasion for asking the searching, crucial questions.

And it is more too. It is a day which summons us to repair what has been broken, to retrace the steps that have gone astray, to undo while time yet remains and as opportunity permits, the wrongs we are doing to others and to ourselves.

This is the day which urges us in the words of the contemporary poet, Stephen Spender:

> Never to allow gradually the traffic to smother
> With noise and fog the flowering of the spirit.

Above all, this is the day which whispers to each of us with divine insistence: Your primary duty is to find yourself! You must not get lost in the world!

FINDING OURSELVES

Throughout the year that lies ahead, may God keep us faithful to that summons and to the prayer we now utter:

O Thou who art from everlasting to everlasting, who makest all things new and yet abidest forever the same,

Thou hast fashioned us as frail creatures of time and hast put a hunger for eternity in our hearts. On the gateway to a New Year we have come before Thy presence to seek Thee and in seeking Thee to find ourselves.

Above the din of a noisy world speak to us with the still, small voice of Thy spirit.

If our lives have become shallow, deepen them.

If our principles have become shabby, repair them.

If our ideals have become tarnished, restore them.

If our hopes have become faded, revive them.

If our loyalties have grown dim, brighten them.

If our values have become confused, clarify them.

If our purposes have grown blurred, sharpen them.

If our horizons have become contracted, widen them.

Be Thou the North Star of our lives and may the compass of conscience help us to steer an honorable course.

In the words of those who go down to the sea in ships, we pray: Keep us, O God, for our boat is small and the ocean wide.

THE FINE ART OF LETTING GO

So many of our most cherished possessions—including life itself—belong to us very briefly. Too soon they are gone. This
sober truth need not depress us. It can actually help us to
deepen and enrich our lives.

Preached on Yom Kippur, 1956

8

The Fine Art of Letting Go

YIZKOR IS RECITED four times during the Jewish calendar year—on each of the three festivals and on Yom Kippur. On three festivals one cannot but feel somewhat uncomfortable with the intrusion of the solemn Yizkor mood. In the midst of a symphony of Yom Tov joy, it strikes the jarring note of sorrow. It seems somewhat reminiscent of the practice among some ancient peoples of dangling a skeleton at a feast.

But on Yom Kippur, the Yizkor theme seems to blend so naturally into the motif of this day. The mood of this day is one of renunciation, of surrendering. We give up food and drink and a host of other pleasures in which we normally indulge. The Yizkor hour completes the thought by reminding us that life invariably demands of us the most difficult of all surrenders—the surrender of loved ones. Some of us are today reciting the Yizkor for a loved one for the first time, the most painful time of all. Others have grown familiar with the prayer through repeated usage. To all of us, this hour drives home vividly the melancholy truth of the wise man's admonition:

> "Remind thyself that he whom thou lovest is mortal—that what thou lovest is not thine own; it is given thee for the present not irrevocably nor forever, but even as a fig or a bunch of grapes at the appointed season."

Yizkor thus strikes a sobering note. At this season when we pray for life and for the things we should like to acquire, Yizkor reminds us that life inevitably also entails relinquishing. It compels us to look upon life not only as an adventure in stock-piling and pyramiding possessions. Life is also a stern teacher whose lesson is accepting restrictions, developing the fine art of letting go. We must learn, in Carl Sandburg's words, "to loosen your hands, let go and say goodbye." And it is not of death alone that I am thinking.

Consider, for example, the inescapable fact that life compels us to let go of our youth with its attendant physical strength and vitality. Our muscles lose their flexibility, our reflexes are slowed, our recuperative powers are diminished.

I wonder how many of us hear an echo of our own complaints in the following protesting piece someone recently wrote: "Everything is farther than it used to be. It's twice as far to the station, for instance, and they've added a hill, I've just noticed. I've given up running for my train; it leaves faster than it used to.

"Seems to me they are making staircases steeper than in the old days. And have you noticed the small print they are using lately? Newspapers are getting farther and farther away when I hold them and I have to squint to make out the news. No sense in asking to have them read aloud: everyone seems to speak in such a low voice I scarcely can hear them.

"The barber doesn't hold a mirror behind me any more so I can see the back of my head. And shoe laces are so short they are all but impossible to reach.

"Even the people are changing. They're so much younger than they used to be when I was their age!

"On the other hand, people my own age are so much older than I am. I ran into an old classmate the other night and he aged so he didn't recognize me. I got to thinking about the poor old fellow while I was shaving this morning. While doing so, I glanced at my own reflection in the mirror. Confound it, they don't even use the same kind of glass in mirrors any more!"

Is there any wonder that as life rolls inexorably forward, where there was once a sense of eager anticipation there is now some hesitancy in the face of tomorrow and a greater tendency to dwell upon yesterday with lingering regret. We pray for old age but how reluctant we are to pay the toll the advancing years exact on the throughway of life.

Life also has a way of compelling us to let go of our children. Our children grow up and away. They develop independence, they try their own wings. That of course is as it should be and we should silently rejoice that we have brought them to that stage. Yet who will deny that their leaving fills us with a certain loneliness and an inner emptiness which is not easily filled. Some of the tears shed under the wedding canopy speak of this sadness. We are no longer needed quite so desperately. To a disquieting extent we have become expendable.

This relinquishing process actually sets in long before our children marry. Our children belong to us only for some very few years in infancy and early childhood. Too soon they become people, they withdraw more and confide less, semi-strangers in the home, whom we can no longer direct, whom we must turn over to life. The more graciously we recognize this, the happier our homes are likely to be. But any parent struggling through the turbulent adolescent years will be quick to testify that this is not an easy task. The three things we owe our children, it has been said, are dedication, education and abdication. Of the three, who will deny that it is the last duty which is the most difficult to discharge? Relinquishing children is by far the most demanding part of rearing them.

And so, in so many vital areas, life sternly demands of us to surrender, to renounce, to relinquish. Loved ones die, youth fades, our children leave us.

Now this is undoubtedly a severe view of life which may induce a drooping of spirit and a flagging of morale. But its purpose is actually to stress an indispensable ingredient for grown-up living. No life has really matured if it has not mastered the fine art of letting go.

Need we spell out in detail the needless grief of those who cannot liberate themselves from the legacy of bereavement left by the death of someone very dear? They are the unfortunate ones for whom the death is re-enacted every day, who permit the birds of sorrow to build a permanent nest in their hearts, who do not permit time to perform its benign act of healing, who walk forever in the shadows and are afraid to face the sunshine. We cannot be severe with such people; we can only feel genuinely sorry for them. If only they had mastered the difficult but desperately needed art of letting go of loved ones.

And what shall we say of those who have not learned to relinquish their youth? In a sense, of course, we are all victims of the commercials which have convinced us that somehow it is wrong to look one's age. If you want to make a life-long enemy just tell a woman that she looks her age. But tell her that she looks like her daughter's girl-friend and you can sell her any dress or hat in the store. The middle aged gay blade who tries to follow a pace of action and a mode of dress which is the envy of his son-in-law, is trying stoutly to convince the world and probably also himself that he has lost none of his vibrant youthfulness. He usually succeeds only in becoming grotesque and ludicrous.

A psychiatrist was recently asked to differentiate between those two oft-used words: psychosis and neurosis. "A psychotic" he said, "thinks that two and two make five. A neurotic, on the other hand, knows that two plus two equals four—but it bothers him."

There are millions of Americans who believe that thirty years and thirty years equals thirty nine, to use a number made very popular by a well-known comedian. This kind of arithmetic is evidence of psychosis. There are others who know that thirty and thirty equals sixty but, oh, how it bothers them! What they show in common is a failure to master the fine art of letting go of youth.

Those who cannot relinquish children are storing up vast reserves of misery which pay dreary dividends with the passing years. Where the parent does not appreciate the vital role of "abdication" in the healthy normal development of the child, the child does not grow from a feeling of dependence with which all life starts into a strong sense of independence and without which mature living is impossible. A keen student of child growth has put the matter very simply: "Parents owe it to their children they bring into the world to put the tools of living into their hands— hands which we have made as strong and as capable as we can. But having given them the hands and the tools, we owe it to them not to do the digging for them."

Where parents fail to heed this sound advice the consequences are often spelled out later on in broken marriages. The wife or husband can not face a challenging situation and resolve it. It is so much easier and more natural to run back to mother. The grown boy may become a financial giant but remain forever an emotional midget. If his rules of the game are not accepted, he picks up the marbles and goes sulking off to his tent. Hartley Coleridge's lines may well serve as his epitaph:

> And still I am a child
> Though I grow old.

Exorbitant indeed is the price to be paid for failure to master the fine art of letting go of children.

Yes, Yizkor time on Yom Kippur is a most appropriate moment for absorbing one of the basic lessons of life—the need for relinquishing, for letting go.

But if that were all this day taught us, it should only serve to make us sadder for having been here. The true purpose of this hour, however, is quite otherwise. After the Psalmist considered soberly and realistically the nature of our lives he prayed, "Teach us to number our days that we may acquire a heart of wisdom." The purpose of this accounting is to make us wiser, to make us better.

The awareness that life dictates that we surrender so much that is so very precious to us should spur us on to enjoy these very things while they are ours, to clasp them to our breast with warm embrace. Because we and those we love are mortal, we ought to love each other powerfully while we may, and serve each other with added tenderness. Because life is of limited duration, ours is the task to make it of unlimited depth. Because its quantity is fixed, we should enrich its quality.

Rabbi Joshua Loth Liebman died young, much too young for a man who had so much to give. There is therefore added significance to the following words he wrote not too long before his death:

"And while we live, we should try to make each day a year as far as beauty, nobility, and a warm sense of brotherhood are concerned. In a time when there is so much cruelty abroad, we must generate the oxygen of love to keep the soul of the world still breathing. Religion should summon all of us to treasure each other in the recognition that we do not know how long we shall have each other. The crimes and sins for which there should be little forgiveness are hardheartedness, selfishness, mutual cruelty, lovelessness—all of the little weapons which we use to shorten the lives of others. Our very understanding of each other can serve to deepen life even when we cannot lengthen it."

Yes, youth fades but may it be ours to use it well while it is ours. Let us husband it and preserve it well. Let us not squander it recklessly nor spend it in such a way as to bequeath a burden of guilt to our later years. "Well-spent is our youth" our sages remind us "if it does not embarrass our old age."

THE FINE ART OF LETTING GO

And let us remember too that the later years do have their own joys and satisfactions. Let us learn to look for them, they are there! God has so arranged our lives that every age has its uniquely rich compensations. Let us not foolishly fail to grasp the joys at hand because they are not the same joys we experienced twenty years ago. For that matter neither do we have now the worries, the anxieties, the doubts we had then.

> Let me grow lovely growing old
> So many fine things to do
> Laces and ivory and gold
> And silks need not be new
> And there is healing in old trees
> Old streets a glamour hold
> Why may not I as well as these
> Grow lovely, growing old?
>
> (*Karle Wilson Baker*)

Yes, our children grow up and away. Let us enjoy them while we have them. Let us not be absentee parents. Let us not concentrate so hard on acquiring needless luxuries for them that we fail to give them their greatest necessity—a piece of ourselves. And if we love them properly, we shall have helped them to become more lovable not only by ourselves but by every one whose life they touch and bless.

You see, dear friends, when we truly master the art of letting go, we have enormously increased our opportunities for enjoying our bounties while they are ours. And this fundamentally is the true function of these Holy Days.

There is one more aspect to our theme, dear friends, with which I should like to complete it.

The realization that we and ours are here only briefly is a challenge to us to identify ourselves with something which will endure after we are gone. Because we are perishable, we ought to try to become part of the things which are imperishable. "The great use of life," William James has finely said, "is to spend it for something that will outlast it."

In our daily morning service, we read an interesting passage from the Mishnah. It reads as follows:

"The following are mitzvot whose fruits a man enjoys in this life while the principal remains his to all eternity: honoring father and mother, performing deeds of loving kindness, attending the house of study morning and evening, extending hospitality to wayfarers, visiting the sick, providing a dowry for a needy bride, paying final respects to the dead, devotion in prayer, and the making of peace between man and his fellowman. And the study of Torah is equivalent to them all."

What does this Mishnah say to us—and say it, mind you—every day of our lives, if we pray? It tells us that these acts not only bring pleasure to us when we perform them, but the principal, the deed itself, is something which is eternally ours. We take on an aspect of eternity as we promote undying good. The kind man dies but his act of kindness is indestructible. The man who visits the sick is mortal but his act of having visited the sick, has linked him to something which is immortal. The student of the Torah passes away but his act of study can never pass away. "Every good deed is a thread of gold in the tapestry of eternity." What our tradition teaches us therefore is that we are as immortal as the things with which we join our lives.

For me, personally, there are so many blessings in being a Jew but chief among them is the realization that as I link my life and my efforts to an eternal people, my life thereby becomes part of something so much more enduring than one man's life. Being a Jew has given me a sparkling opportunity to spend my life for something that will outlast it.

THE FINE ART OF LETTING GO

And so we face this *Yizkor* hour, soberly mindful of life's heavy demands and also of its enormous challenges. Let it inspire us so to live that others, remembering our lives in the years to come, will draw from them the courage to spend their days wisely and to invest a portion of them, in the things that never die.

FOR THE SIN WE HAVE SINNED

At a time when there appears to be a widespread "stampede away from responsibility" the central message of Yom Kippur has a crucial relevance. It reminds us that we are indeed morally responsible creatures. This has vital implications for our tomorrows and also for our todays.

Preached on Kol Nidre, 1959

9

For the Sin We Have Sinned

IN THE *Amidah*, just concluded, we recited the *Al Chet*, the confessional which occupies the most prominent part in the Yom Kippur prayers. The reason why the enumeration of our sins is given so much space on the spiritual landscape of this day is to be found in the fact that the confessional underscores the basic theme of Yom Kippur. When we say, *al chet shechatanu*, "for the sin which we have sinned," we accept responsibility for our deeds and misdeeds. And our tradition bids us to repeat this recitation again and again in order to drive home the heavy truth we are so reluctant to accept—that we are responsible for our actions.

This truth is not too popular in our times.

When Russia recently announced that it had sent a rocket to the moon, the reaction in America was relatively mild. But when Russia successfully launched its first sputnik, on October 4, 1957, it triggered an era of excruciating self-examination here in America. We who had always believed that we had the most of the best of everything, including scientific genius and know-how, were stunned by the Soviet achievement. When the passage of a little time dulled the sharp blow to our collective ego, we began to ask ourselves why had America forfeited its world scientific leadership? Where had we erred?

Many explanations were offered. One of the most incisive diagnoses of our condition was made in a speech by one Charles H. Brower, whose words were subsequently reprinted in several national magazines. Mr. Brower explained America's failure in these words:

"This period in America is the high tide of mediocrity, the great era of the 'goof off,' the age of the half done job. The land from coast to coast has been enjoying a stampede away from responsibility.

"It is populated with laundry men who won't iron shirts, with waiters who won't serve, with carpenters who will come around some day maybe, with executives whose minds are on the golf course, with students who take cinch courses because the hard ones make them think, with spiritual delinquents of all kinds, who have triumphantly determined to enjoy what was known until the present crisis as 'the new leisure.' . . . Unquestionably we are in a battle for survival. We must get our people into the battle. But first we have to get some battle into the people."

Tonight, dear friends, I want to deal with another phase of what Mr. Brower called "a stampede away from responsibility." I want to speak not of our economic responsibility, or educational responsibility, but of our moral responsibility. It is of this responsibility that we speak throughout this day of Yom Kippur when we say we have sinned . . . we have dealt treacherously. We accept responsibility for our deeds and misdeeds.

This major premise of Yom Kippur is quite at variance with the dominant mood of our time which relieves man of responsibility for his actions. Morally speaking, we are enjoying a stampede away from responsibility.

A teenage delinquent recently complained to a psychologist that her only feeling of guilt stemmed from the fact that despite her impressive list of misdeeds she felt no sense of guilt. The truth is that the contemporary moral climate makes it extremely difficult for a man to say: "I have sinned." Indeed, the very word "sin" has an old-fashioned, archaic ring. To sin implies that we have committed a wrong but we are not prepared to blame ourselves.

Who is to blame? Often we say that it is the environment that is guilty. It is so tempting to blame conditions and circumstances. In Buffalo, N. Y. a 16 year old boy was killed in an automobile accident. His father went to court to obtain the right to put the following inscription on the boy's tombstone. "In memory of our beloved son—a victim of the present social system and the conditions it creates." One of the father's arguments was that the social system in the United States "has ended parental authority over their children." As the trial unfolded, the father's attorney admitted that the boy had been drinking and was racing with some other boys when the fatal accident happened. One is sorely tempted to conclude that it was not the social system at all that was to blame.

When we are not blaming society for our misdemeanors, we are likely to shift the responsibility to our emotional or psychological conditioning. We have picked up enough of the current jargon of the psychiatrist to provide ample escape hatches from our guilt feeling. As children we may have felt unwanted. Perhaps there was intense sibling rivalry or frustration or maladjustment. We are a bundle of complexes, reflexes, fixations. It is any or all of these which are responsible for our misbehavior—not we.

In the musical play *West Side Story*, which portrays the ugly, deadly warfare between New York City's teenage gangs, one such gang is trying to explain in song to Officer Krupke why it acts as it does. The explanation is an acute reflection of one of our most popular escapes from moral responsibility. Listen to the words:

> "Dear, kindly Sergeant Krupke
> You gotta understand.
> It's just our bringing upke
> That gets us outa hand.

Our mothers all are junkies
Our fathers all are drunks
Golly, Moses, naturally we're punks."

This type of self-exoneration is not limited to the young. Some time back, a bank director embezzled something like $1,000,000 from the National City Bank of New York. When he was captured in Florida, he said: "I don't know why I did it. Maybe a good psychiatrist or two can figure it out." Notice the total evasion of responsibility. He was not to blame. Some mysterious subterranean forces were at work compelling him to steal. Let the psychiatrist figure out where to put the blame. The culprit you see had a built in alibi to shield him against responsibility.

Another echo of the same thinking is found in Eugene O'Neill's *Long Day's Journey Into Night*, which paints a dreary picture of an entire modern family going to seed. Moral decay overtakes each in turn. The mother is addicted to dope, the father to drink. The sons are each sick with another spiritual malady. It is a family without roots, without love, without any sustaining vitality. But perhaps one of the saddest lines in the story, is the mother's pathetic effort to lighten their burden of responsibility for the deterioration which has set in. "None of us can help the things life has done to us," she says. "They are done before you realize it and before you know it you have lost yourself forever." Notice the mood of helplessness. We are powerless against the forces of life.

The truth is that man's effort to avoid moral responsibility for his actions is not a distinctively modern phenomenon. It seems to be as old as man himself. When Adam in the garden eats from the forbidden tree and God confronts him with the accusing question: "Hast thou eaten of the tree, whereof I commanded thee that thou shouldst not eat?" what does Adam answer? "The woman whom Thou gavest to be with me, she gave me of the tree and I did eat." Notice what Adam is doing. He is dividing the blame equally between the Almighty and the woman. "The woman whom Thou gavest me"—I didn't ask for her. She was your idea and your creation. "She gave me of the tree"—the eating was her idea not mine.

Now, Adam might have been the first husband to blame his wife for his own misdeeds but there may be one or two women in the congregation tonight who will testify that he was definitely not the last. Before the ladies start feeling very superior about this matter I ought to point out that evading moral responsibility is not strictly a masculine affliction. In that same biblical incident God turns to Eve after Adam passes the moral buck to her and asks: "What is this thou hast done?" Not to be outdone, Eve replies: "The serpent beguiled me and I did eat."

Evasion of responsibility is one of our most persistent human traits. Every age provides its own Eves and its own serpents. Today we are pictured as the victims of genes, reflexes, complexes, passions, glands. It is biology and heredity and sociology and psychology each revealing massive forces which buffet us about and which you and I are impotent to control. In an earlier, less sophisticated age when men believed in astrology, it was the heavenly bodies which served as the Eves and the serpents. Do you remember Edmund's description of that kind of buck passing in Shakespeare's *King Lear?*

"This is the excellent foppery of the world, that when we are sick in fortune—often the surfeit of our own behavior—we make guilty of our disasters the sun, the moon and the stars: as if we were villains by necessity, fools by heavenly compulsion; knaves, thieves and treachers by spherical predominance; drunkards, liars and adulterers, by an enforced obedience of planetary influence. . . ."

Man has always sought and found someone or something to serve as his whipping boy, to carry the burden of responsibility

105

and guilt he was unwilling to assume. Man committed the deed, but only as a robot, a puppet. The real mover was something outside of himself. This whole philosophy of evasion was neatly summed up in a recent cartoon in which a little boy complains to his father: "Mother is always blaming me for everything I do." We want to do what we will but we want our Eves and our serpents to take the blame.

Along comes Yom Kippur and bars the exits by which we escape from moral responsibility. It neatly catalogues our sins, bids us repeat them to the point of weariness and in so doing places the blame precisely where it belongs—upon my shoulders and yours.

We are not robots or puppets. We are free moral agents, capable of choosing between right and wrong. "I call heaven and earth to witness against you this day, that I have set before thee life and death, the blessing and the curse; therefore choose life, that thou mayest live, thou and thy seed."

This is not to deny the vital influence exercised upon us by our biological inheritance, our childhood experiences, our environmental conditioning. These things are real and powerful but the human will is even more powerful. For man is not only shaped by his environment; he shapes it. Man is not only the creature of circumstance. He is the creator of circumstance. Man not only reacts, he also responds and the crucial factor is the nature of his response.

Our genes may determine whether our eyes are blue or brown —but whether we look with envy or compassion depends upon us.

Our physical height may be biologically determined before we are born but our human stature we ourselves fashion.

Our environment determines the language we speak and the pronunciation we use but whether our words are cruel or gentle, critical or comforting is the result of our own free choice.

Passions and appetites and instincts are part of our animal

equipment but whether they rule us or we rule them is left for each of us to determine.

The classic Jewish position was put most forthrightly by Maimonides: "God does not decree that a man should be good or evil. It is only fools and ignoramuses among Gentiles and Jews who maintain this nonsense. Any man born is free to become as righteous as Moses, as wicked as Jeroboam, a student or an ignoramus, kind or cruel, generous or niggardly." However we are tempted to excuse ourselves, in our heart of hearts, we recognize this truth. We know that we are free to choose.

And, contrary to the widespread misconception, modern psychology endorses this point of view.

Only recently I read an article by a clinical psychologist, Dr. Julius Segal, called, "That Old-Fashioned Will Power," in which the author decries the tendency of people to slough off personal responsibility. He hammers home the point that while psychologists can tell us more about ourselves than ever before, while they can help lay bare hidden motives, we must understand that we have the power to act on our own and the responsibility to use that power. We have to reassert that old fashioned will power.

Thus the most modern insights into the heart of man confirm the basic theme of our tradition which runs through the entire liturgy of this day. We are morally responsible for our deeds because we are morally free to choose.

But when we have said all this we have not yet fully exhausted the meaning of this day. There is a second side to the coin of moral freedom. Because we are free to choose, we are not only responsible for our past, but we are also capable of changing our course in the future. We can give new direction to our lives. We are not eternally chained by what we have been. We can throw off the tyranny of debasing habits. Our tomorrow can be freed from the shackles of yesterday.

This is the meaning of T'shuvah, repentance. It is compounded of remorse for what we have been, and resolve to be what we are free to become. To believe in the power of *T'shuvah* means to affirm that we can conquer the envy which gnaws at us, the selfishness which shrinks us, the prejudice which blinds us, the passion which enslaves us, the indifference which dehumanizes us.

"How do we know that a man's sins have been forgiven?" asked a Hassidic rabbi. And he answered. "When he no longer commits the sin." We are free to break with what we have been; to be what the better angels of our nature assure us we can become.

And in this struggle we are not alone. God is our ally. God who gave us the power to repent helps us in this endeavor. Our sages picture God as saying to us: "If you open the door of repentance only as wide as a needle's eye, I will open it wide enough to permit carriages and wagons to pass through." God helps those who want to remake themselves, to refine their character, to redirect their lives.

In brief then this is the two-fold meaning of this day: responsibility for yesterday, opportunity for tomorrow. But the choice must be made today.

"Behold I set before you the choice today." God grant us the will to choose, and the wisdom to choose wisely.

ISRAEL REVISITED

For the Jew, Israel is more than a piece of geography. It is history, theology, memory, anguish and ecstasy, childhood legends and daily prayers. Some of the astonishing achievements of the fledgling State, as well as the formidable problems that still confront it, are sketched from the perspective of one who sees the land after a lapse of six years.

Preached on Rosh Hashanah, 1961

10

Israel Revisited

SIX YEARS AGO on Rosh Hashanah I shared with the congregation my impressions of the State of Israel after a visit of more than four leisurely months. During the past summer, I had the privilege of revisiting the Holy Land, this time for only several weeks. Today I should like to tell you about the Israel I saw this summer, some of the impressive changes that have been wrought since our last pilgrimage, and some of the challenges that confront the State which has just celebrated its Bar Mitzvah and thus crossed the invisible line which divides childhood from maturity.

Before we talk about what the eye sees in Israel, we must first record what the heart feels because it is in the hunger of the heart that an *aliyah* to Israel begins. The American Jew who goes to visit Israel is drawn not by a desire to see beautiful scenery, although Israel is enchantingly beautiful. What draws him to Israel is an inner longing, a powerful craving to tread upon soil which for him has a unique appeal, an almost mystic magnetism.

What Cleveland Amory has written about Boston, I would apply to Israel. "Boston," he said "is not only a city. It is a state of mind." For the Jew, Israel is a state of mind. It is not only a piece of geography. It is history. It is theology. It is memory. It is Jewish tears and Jewish triumphs. It is Jewish anguish and Jewish ecstasy. It is childhood legends and Biblical verses. It is the direction that we pray and the subject of our prayers. It is exile and home-coming. It is a burning **Temple and** a new flag at the United Nations. It is *Tisha B'Av* and *Yom Atzmaut.*

So although we shall be talking of the things we can see and measure and count and describe, we must bear in mind throughout that there is behind it all a very special state of mind which we feel in Israel and nowhere else and which defies capture by words. Those who have been to Israel will know what I mean; the others will understand when they get there.

A clue to this feeling is found in the British War Cemetery on the outskirts of Beer Sheba, which was the first town captured by General Allenby's men from the Turks in 1917, during the first World War. The British soldiers who fell in this battle lie buried at the approach to the city. Among them there is one Jewish captain. Upon his grave, there is this inscription: "So far and yet so near to home." Far away from Britain and yet so near to home! So many Jewish tourists report a strange feeling of being at home in Israel, at home in a land they have never before seen with their own eyes. And so over and above everything else, Israel is a state of mind which gives every moment spent there an added dimension of awareness experienced nowhere else.

The dominant impression that Israel stamps upon the visitor immediately is that this little country is just bursting with energy, jumping with dynamic creativity. *Es tut zich!* All about you, roads are being built, pipe-lines are being laid, rocky soil is being cleared, homes are being erected. Cranes, tractors, bulldozers hum their incessant music on every side.

When Dore Schary was asked to describe Israel he said that the most fitting word was *vitality*. "Israel fizzes with it. It's like living in a glass of Alka-Seltzer."

To fully appreciate the "fizz" of Israel you have to visit Europe too. There everything is completed and done. It was finished a long time ago. When you tour Europe you are shown the legacy of the slumbering centuries—the art, the architecture, the historic shrines and landmarks of yesterday. Your guide uses almost exclusively the past tense. In Israel, although it is hallowed by so many memories, your guide keeps talking future tense. You know you are part of an emerging society, a land in the making. Everything is becoming. Tomorrow there will be a factory here, a new port here, a tree here, a railroad track here, a new village here. Tomorrow! You live with a sense of expectancy, with a sense of impatience. And as our sages tell us: V'haya—"wherever Scripture uses future tense—'And it shall come to pass'—that is a good omen." Wherever the stress falls on what is yet to be, there is hope, there is buoyancy, there is, in short, a fizz.

Israel's anticipations for the future are nourished by its achievements in the past. In 1955, the highway that leads from Haifa to Tel Aviv was almost completely exposed to the burning sun with virtually no relief. Today it is largely sheltered and shaded by trees on both sides of it. In some places the trees are so thick you can scarcely see the fields behind them. Stony stretches of bleak land have been covered by green carpets—hill to hill carpeting. Land is not only being reclaimed. It is almost being created anew. When you see things grow in the most forbidding places, you are tempted to recite a new bracha: Hamotzi adamah min ha'aretz. Blessed art Thou who gives our people the faith and the courage and the love to bring forth living soil from the barren land.

The landscape has been changed in other ways too. The once naked mountains to the west of Jerusalem now carry Hadassah's new 30 million dollar hospital, one of the world's greatest medical centers. It was built there, although it is six miles from the center of Jerusalem, in response to an appeal from Israel's prime minister, Ben Gurion. For security reasons, he wanted to solidify the western approaches to Jerusalem. By building its hospital where it did, Hadassah also gave momentum to the westward development of Jerusalem in the corridor towards Tel Aviv. It is already being linked to Jerusalem by a breath-taking chain of new housing projects and intermediate villages of Rassco, Katamon, Malcha,

Kiryat Hayovel, Ir Ganim and Ein Karem. Around the 300 acre medical center itself a town to be called Kiryat Hadassah will be built for the hospital employees.

From the Hadassah Hospital looking southward we see the magnificent spacious and functional buildings of the Hebrew University, all built since our last visit. A little further along we see the new government buildings, some already completed and others including the new Knesset structure, in various stages of construction. In Jerusalem itself the buildings seem to have grown taller. When you ask someone, "Why do the buildings seem bigger now than they did six years ago?" they tell you: "Because they are!" They have actually been building additional stories on top of existing buildings.

And so it goes throughout the country. The Weizmann Institute in Rehovot has grown powerfully, to house its departments for Applied Mathematics, Biophysics, Electronics, Experimental Biology, Isotope Research, Optics, Organic Chemistry, Physics, Microbology and Plant Genetics. The institute also has the only electronic brain in the Middle East.

The growth of the Weizmann Institute has been matched by the development of the Technion, Israel's M.I.T. on the slope of Mt. Carmel. Outside of Tel Aviv, there has been built Bar Ilan University on the same philosophy as Yeshiva University in New York City.

When the State was born thirteen years ago, Beer Sheba was a little village of some 5,000 Arab Bedouins. Today it is a flourishing city of 50,000 inhabitants which has arisen out of the desert sands to become Israel's proud capital of the Negev.

In the Book of Kings we read: "And King Solomon made a navy of ships in Ezion-Geber which is beside Elath on the shore of the Red Sea. . . ." (II Kings 9:26) Eilat, on the southern tip of Israel, was a well-known city in the Biblical period. In the time of the British mandate, however, there was only a small mud-brick police station to relieve the desolation. Before the Sinai campaign Eilat had a population of some 3 or 4 hundred. When Israel's army opened the Gulf of Eilat to Israel shipping, thus giving Israel a gateway to Africa and the Far East, Eilat came into its own. It now has a population of some 7,000 and according to our local guide, every month on schedule, 20 new babies are born. Israel calls this *aliyah p'nimit*, internal immigration.

One of Eilat's most important sources of revenue are the nearby copper mines of King Solomon which had been idle for 3,000 years. Using the Bible as a guide and remembering the description of the Promised Land found in Deuteronomy (5:9) "a land whose stones are iron and out of whose hills thou mayest dig brass," Israel has discovered the ancient sources of copper and is today exploiting them. Already the mines are earning nearly 4 million dollars a year. Within five years they are expected to produce an annual profit of 10 million dollars.

A heartening change in Israel's landscape has been the virtual disappearance of the *ma'abarot*, the frail immigrant huts which were such a sad sight in 1955. Outside of Tel Aviv we passed warehouses where the dismantled shacks, the corrugated tin roofs were piled, being readied for other uses. Today the immigrant does not go from the ship or plane to a demoralizing *ma'abarah* for an indefinite sojourn. He goes directly from the ship to a home in a new village which is waiting for him.

Some of the most vital changes that are taking place in Israel are not visible to the naked eye. They are changes that take place inside of people. They involve such things as dignity and freedom and self-respect and equality.

An elderly Jew as he was about to enter the polling booth in the recent elections, was heard reciting the *Shehechiyanu*. As he came out, he was asked why he did so. "I come from behind the Iron Curtain," he answered.

On the outskirts of Jerusalem you come to a small Yemenite

settlement. You see some fruits and vegetables growing. You see a man riding on a horse. You see modest-looking houses, a barn, a few chicken coops, a general store. Altogether an unspectacular sight. Statistically, it is one more new settlement. But in human terms nothing less than a revolution has taken place in this community. The Yemenite Jew comes from a country where he never was permitted to own a piece of land. He did not even work on the soil. Moreover, he was forbidden to ride on a horse because he was not allowed to be able to look down on a Moslem. (For the same reason he was not permitted to build a house above a certain height.) When he saw an Arab approaching on a horse he had to step aside and yield the right of way. Now this Jew owns land, makes it productive, rides a horse, helps determine who is to be the next Prime Minister, is protected by law. He has become a human being.

Another area of spectacular progress in Israel has been in the field of science. Israel's scientific sophistication made headlines throughout the world early in July when Israel fired Shavit II, a rocket completely manufactured in Israel by Israelis. Thus a nation of 2 million joined the exclusive rocket club which includes only the United States, Russia, Britain, France, Japan and Italy. But there are other vital scientific and technical achievements which have not made headlines. An Israeli scientist has invented a new process for making "heavy water," which is necessary for producing atomic power. Remarkable progress has been made in Israel in harnessing solar energy. Many Israeli households are already equipped with solar energy devices to produce hot water during Israel's 8-month summer. The work being done at the Negev Institute for Arid Zone Research is so promising that it has received financial support from UNESCO and from the Ford and Rockefeller Foundations.

Perhaps most hopeful for the future of Israel and for the future of all of humanity is Israel's desalination work known as the

Zarchin Process after the Russian Jewish scientist who discovered it.

If Israel can succeed in recovering fresh water from the sea at a price which makes it economically feasible it will have scored one of the great breakthroughs in man's struggle for survival. The Chicago American has written: "Discovering a cheap way to make sea water fresh is an event of incalculable importance to the world . . . the inventor of the machine, Alexander Zarchin may go down in history as one of the great benefactors of humanity." Israel may very well be remembered by posterity for having turned the sea into a well that never runs dry. In our Psalms we extoll God who took water out of the rock, "Who converted the rock into a stream of water." If Israel can convert the sea into a stream of fresh water, it will have accomplished its part in the divine partnership.

Our respect for Israel's scientific stature is enormously enhanced when we realize that none of the other newly-created nations have any scientific knowledge at all.

And this leads directly to another achievement whose significance cannot be exaggerated. One of the very exciting developments in Israel is the role it is playing in teaching younger nations how to organize their economy, their agricultural settlements, their communities. These countries are sending their students to Israel to learn, are inviting Israelis to come to their countries to teach them. Requests have come to Israel from Togo, from the Ivory Coast, from the Congo, Upper Volta, from Mali, from Center Africa, Chad, Ghana, Western Nigeria, Eastern Nigeria, Tanganyika, Ethiopia, Uganda, Napal, Burma, Philippines and Cyprus. They are expecting Israel to come and teach them something of the miracle of Israel. Today, Nigeria has 4 Hebrew schools for the children of Israelis who work there. Eye surgery is being performed for the first time in some African countries, thanks to Israeli surgeons who are bringing their skills to these lands. The reason why these people are turning to Israel and not to Russia, America or China, is because they feel that they have more to learn from Israel which is small and like themselves. Six years ago, the entire Lachish area was complete desert. Today it contains a series of villages. One of them is Kiryat Gat. It consists of people who came mainly from Asia and Africa who never engaged in agriculture, many of them never did any manual work, but now 5 years later, they have created a flourishing community. That is why the people of Africa are coming to Israel to learn how it is being done.

Ben Gurion told us that he had recently attended a celebration of Ghanaian independence in Israel. There were a large number of African people present and he talked to them in English, the official language of Ghana. Then one man started to talk to him in perfect fluent Hebrew, and Ben Gurion asked him where he had learned it. He answered that he was a student at the Hebrew University for 4 years. You have finished now, are you going home? No, he said, I want to make a study of plant diseases, so I shall remain on in the agricultural school in Rehovot.

Another notable step forward was taken last month when it was announced that the Hadassah Medical Organization and the Hebrew University will open a complete medical school for Afro-Asian students in Jerusalem in November. Some 20 students have already been enrolled from Nigeria, Liberia, Ghana, Mali and Ethiopia. The World Health Organization considers this venture so important that it is contributing $1000 per student for tuition fees.

For the people of a score of Afro-Asian countries, the ancient prophecy is already being fulfilled: "For out of Zion shall go forth learning and the word of God from Jerusalem."

A most gratifying development which should be noted is that Israel is quickly becoming the central address of the Jewish people and the gathering place for its most vital assemblies. During this past summer alone, the following groups gathered in Israel: the Israel Bond Conference with some 400 delegates; the World Congress of Jewish Studies with some 1000 participants including non-Jewish scholars; the Rabbinical Council of America with some 500 orthodox rabbis, synagogue leaders and their wives; the Zimriya-choral groups from all over the world, including two non-Jewish ones, which gave several concerts and won widest critical acclaim; the World Conference of Physicians which brought some 220 physicians from 19 countries for 10 days of lectures and discussions on medical developments in Israel and abroad. These gatherings symbolize the return of the old crown of learning and culture to Jerusalem, the fountain of the Jewish spirit.

In addition to these adult groups we must call attention to the thousands of Jewish teenagers from America who traveled in groups, touring the country with expert Israeli guides, getting the sand of Israel in their shoes, the sun of Israel on their skins, the song of Israel in their souls, the story of Israel in their minds and, I am sure, the love of Israel in their hearts. Who can calculate the meaning of all this for our future?

On the night of Tisha B'Av we joined the multitudes who went up to Mount Zion, which is the closest you can get in Israel to the site of the ancient Temple which is in Jordanian territory. In every corner, in every nook another group was reading Lamentations, the traditional reading on Tisha B'Av. In one corner on the roof there was a group of six American youngsters huddled together over a few flickering candles which they shielded with their cupped hands against the night wind, listening to one of them who was reading Lamentations in English from a J.P.S. Bible. I couldn't help asking myself: What would these youngsters be doing tonite on a Saturday night in July if they were back home? And having done what they are doing here tonight, is it possible that it will leave no imprint on them? We simply have no way of knowing how profound is the influence Israel is exercising upon those who touch its soil.

These, then, are a few of the more conspicuous signs of Israel's progress during the last several years. It would be delightful if we could conclude here and say this is the whole story. But of course it isn't. Some huge problems remain to torment the little state.

The most formidable of these is the security problem. Despite the quiet that has obtained on Israel's borders since the Sinai campaign, Israel is under no illusions as to the intentions of her hostile neighbors. Even if Israel wanted to forget, radio Cairo would not let her. Regularly the Arabs are reminded that the day of Israel's destruction is drawing close. In the face of these pronouncements, Israel has no choice but to remain fully armed with the best and latest equipment available today and to hope that if a military showdown should occur, the moral and spiritual superiority of the Israeli soldier will compensate for the quantitative superiority of the foe in men and weapons. This military readiness imposes a terrible burden upon the economy of Israel, a burden which Israel must not be left to carry alone.

Another great problem which confronts Israel is to resettle the Negev as Ben Gurion has been urging so insistently. I never realized what Ben Gurion was talking about until we flew over the barren Negev on the way down to Eilat. Then I saw with my own eyes what the problem is. The Negev constitutes 60% of Israel's land surface and contains only 1% of Israel's population. The resettlement of the Negev is of greatest economic importance. It is crucial that Israel make the Negev its own not only on the map but in reality as well. Levi Eshkol, Israel's Finance Minister, said, "If we do not conquer the desert the desert will conquer us, and if we do not go out to the border, the border will come to us." The conquest of the Negev means building cities, it means bringing life and people, men, women and children into the desert, it means building homes for them, building water power and light, it means building highways and railroads, it means planting trees and forests against the scorching sun, it means building schools and synagogues. This is another burden Israel should not be asked to carry alone.

A third problem which confronts Israel is the absorption of immigrants. This year the rate of immigration thus far is twice last year's. While we were in Israel the 1 millionth immigrant since the creation of the State arrived. If he was like 90% of his predecessors, he arrived penniless. With him he brought a host of problems of adjustment and rehabilitation. Israel is the only country in the world with no selective immigration. Any Jew who is allowed to leave his country of origin and wants to settle in Israel is admitted. The broken, the maimed, the wounded, the bruised, the demented, all are welcome.

Dr. Joseph Burg, Israel's Minister of Social Welfare, said to us, "On your Statue of Liberty you have the famous words of Emma Lazarus: 'Give me your tired, your poor, your huddled masses yearning to breathe free, the wretched refuse of your teeming shores.' "Well," he said, "you have the words but Israel has the poor, the wretched refuse. You say 'give me,' but Israel got it."

As a consequence, Israel has a tremendous social welfare program. Israel today has 5,000 blind of whom 90% arrived after the birth of the State. In other words, while the population as a whole trebled the blind increased by 900%.

Less than 1% of Israel's immigrants were farmers or agricultural laborers before they came. But more than ½ of all Israeli settlements are agricultural. This involves an enormous task of re-education. In the overall picture, 75% of the newcomers to Israel have to change their occupation after arriving.

These are only some of the reasons why Israel is a laboratory of social problems and the government spends nearly 10 million dollars annually for the handicapped, for relief work and for professional training. This is another burden we have no right to ask Israel to carry alone.

Any Jew must respond with pride at the sight his eyes behold in Israel but there is a special satisfaction which comes to those of us who see it and feel that we have had some share, however modest, in the making of these things. If our hands have not removed the rocks, our dollars have helped, and our money has labored side by side with the sturdy pioneers who are clearing a path in the wilderness.

As your rabbi I felt deeply gratified at the thought that for the last several years we have been setting aside some time during the High Holy Days to consider Israel's needs and to express our sense of solidarity with our brothers across the seas by purchasing Israel Bonds.

Today, dear friends, I think that all of us who are at all able to do so, will want to invest in the future of our people by participating in the Israel Development Loan.

Speaking to us one night at the Kibbutz Maaleh Hahamishah, Ben Gurion said: "Lending money is an old Jewish business but it is only in the last decade that the Jews have had the privilege of lending money to a sovereign Jewish State." And may I add, that never has Jewish money been able to produce such life-giving results and bring such blessings.

On Mount Herzl overlooking Jerusalem those who fell in Israel's War of Liberation lie in their quiet beds of stone. On their granite pillows, their names and ages are recorded. One inscription reads as follows:

Nissin Ginny
The son of Miriam and Yitzchok
was born in Jerusalem

He fell in the fulfillment
of his duty on the 17th of
Iyar 5708
He was 10 years old when he fell.

Nissin Ginny did his duty as he saw it. Let us do ours.

THE JUDGED AND THE JUDGES

Rosh Hashanah, the Day of Judgment, is a good time to face up to the truth that we are not only the judged, we are also the judges. We are constantly passing crucial judgments. Too often we are likely to misjudge. A few words of caution are in order. We might also heed some markers our tradition has posted along the road.

Preached on Rosh Hashanah, 1952
Appeared in The Jewish Exponent, 1953

11

The Judged and the Judges

IN HIS ESSAY "The Over-Soul," Ralph Waldo Emerson wrote: "Our faith comes in moments, our vice is habitual. Yet there is a depth in those brief moments which constrains us to ascribe more reality to them than to all other experiences." For us of the household of American Israel, the present exalted mood of these holy days constitutes such a moment of faith to which Emerson referred. All too infrequently during the year do we find ourselves in this reverent attitude yet who among us will deny that these are the greatest moments in our year? Now we are closer to the heart of the human enterprise, now we more nearly approximate the finest within ourselves, now we are engaged in life's most sacred dialogue, the human soul in communion with its God.

These are not only real moments. They are also solemn moments because in the picturesque language of the prayer-book, we are standing before the divine bar of justice. Today the Great Judge holds court and all His creatures pass in review. He reviews not only our deeds, He also pays attention to motives. "He searches the heart on the Day of Judgment." Who can pass such rigid moral scrutiny without genuine humility and deep remorse?

The truth of the matter is of course that we are judged not only on this *Yom Hadin*—this supreme Day of Judgment. Rabbi Yosi said: "Man is judged daily." Rabbi Nathan went further: "Man is judged every hour." And I should like to go a step further. We are not only judged constantly, but we are constantly judging. And on this Day of Judgment I should like to dwell upon these vital areas where we the judges are so prone to misjudge.

Consider in the first place how prone we are to misjudge our fellowman. All too often we are superficial, impressed by externals, focusing attention upon what a man has rather than what he is. We are like the beggar who approached a kindly-looking gentleman and proceeded to make a moving plea for a contribution. When he had completed his woeful tale, the gentleman said softly: "My friend, I have no money, but I can give you some good advice." The beggar looked at him with contempt. "If you ain't got no money I reckon your advice ain't worth hearing." How many of us use the same reckoning, confusing a man's valuables for his value and his wealth for his worth.

In addition to being superficial in our judgment of others we are too frequently superficial, quick to impugn motives and misinterpret deeds. This is a sin from which, as this morning's haftarah testifies, even the greatest are not exempt. We recall how the tormented Hannah came to the temple to pour out her embittered heart before God. She prayed silently, only her lips moving. And Eli, the high priest, misjudges her anguished movements and taunts her: "How long will you remain drunk? Go put away your wine." And Hannah answers, "No, my lord, I am a woman of a sorrowful spirit, I have drunk neither wine nor strong drink, but I poured out my soul before the Lord." Scripture charitably does not record how Eli felt when he heard that soft reply.

A somewhat similar type of incident is described in a modern poem by Rosa Zagnoni Marinoni which may hit a little closer home because it deals with the super-critical motorist. I have often wondered why our most primitive instincts come to the fore when we drive the most modern vehicle. The title of the poem is "Crushed Fender." The poet was driving one night down a narrow street in Milan when she crashed into another car.

THE JUDGED AND THE JUDGES

I hurled my ire against the guilty one:
"You should be taught to signal as you turn!
At least put out your arm!" I cried at him.
You could have caused our car to overturn!"

At first the man was silent, then he spoke
"Sorry," he said, "to cause you such alarm.
You did not see it, for the night is dark,
But as I turned, I did put out my arm.

Please take my license number and my name
    I hope you will forgive and understand.
I was a soldier once, somewhere in France,
    My left arm is a stub. I have no hand."

I could not speak .The words choked in my throat—
I did not take his number, nor his name—
I turned the car against the dull black night,
My face averted to conceal my shame.

Those whom we misjudge do not usually get the opportunity to defend themselves. Would we therefore not do well to pray in the words of the Sioux Indians: "Great Spirit, help me never to judge another until I have walked two weeks in his moccasins." Ought we not to search diligently for the good in others, humbled by the realization that they may have to search even harder to find the good in us? It is this charitable motivation which prompted our sages to say—"Judge not thy fellow-man until thou art in his place." Until we understand his fears and his frustrations, his hopes and his hungers—until we know all that, we ought not to judge for we are too liable to misjudge.

Consider now in the second place how prone we are to misjudge ourselves. An old Yiddish folk expression has it that "No one will fool you as well as you will fool yourself." If there is anyone we should know well, it is ourselves. Yet modern psychiatry has underscored the truth of the Yiddish expression. We do persistently delude ourselves. Our basest acts often mask themselves to appear like noble deeds. We throw the mantle of deception over our failures so that others and not we must assume the blame.

We did not get the promotion we had hoped for, not because our work left something to be desired, but because "the boss had a grudge against me. He knows I'm superior to him."

We do not succeed in establishing a harmonious relationship with our mates not because we have not really tried hard enough or patiently enough, but because "She doesn't understand me . . . He doesn't understand me."

We do not respond to an appeal for funds from the synagogue, the Seminary or the United Appeal even though we are financially able to do so, not because we are too small to assume our Jewish obligations, but because, "that's all they do, ask for money. Besides I don't like to be asked."

We do not read a book of Jewish content from one year to the next, not because the traditional Jewish love for learning has departed from us, but because in this age of unprecedented leisure, "I just don't have the time."

We who leave our homes three or four nights a week for social and recreational purposes cannot get to services on Friday night, not because we are spiritually indifferent, but because, "after a day's work I'm just too tired."

We who pride ourselves on the attractiveness of our homes have stripped them of the beautiful Jewish rituals and ceremonial objects, not because we are careless custodians of a proud heritage, but because they are old fashioned and our homes modern.

Need we go on? If we were honest with ourselves we could find impressive evidence of our tendency to misjudge ourselves.

Rabbi Yisroel Salanter, whose biography can now be read in English, used to say that the Almighty created us with two eyes so that with one we might observe the virtues of our fellowman while with the other we ought to observe our own limitations and shortcomings. Unfortunately we have reversed the function of our eyes. The eye meant for detecting faults we have trained upon our fellow man. This eye works so well that we can see faults in others where they do not exist. The eye designed for beholding virtue we have trained upon ourselves. This eye also works very well. It looks at weakness and sees strength.

Our reluctance to acknowledge our many failings is exceeded only by our tendency to exaggerate our few virtues.

It is told that the great Sarah Bernhardt was among some friends, when one of them remarked about the strange manner in which some young lady had been acting of late.

"I know why," explained the French actress. "Someone told her that she had a beautiful profile and ever since she has been trying to live sideways."

How many of us live "sideways." How we shriek for the spotlight upon our virtues. How much wiser we would be if we paid more attention to our weaknesses and tried to bring them to the level of our potential strength. The advice of Oliver Cromwell is especially relevant. "A portrait should include all the warts." Only as we have the honesty and the courage to see ourselves with our blemishes, can we outgrow the things that we should leave behind and draw closer to the things to which Rosh Hashanah calls us.

In the last place, on this day when we pray for life, let us consider the sad fact that very often we misjudge the purpose of life and its meaning.

To some degree I believe that all of us have a share in the vulgarization of the human spirit which was perhaps inevitable in an age which has seen wanton destruction of life through Nazi barbarism, world wars, and atomic bombs. As life became cheap, things became precious. That may be why we so often by-pass the lasting things for the latest things.

We sacrifice health for wealth and then try in vain to undo

a bad bargain. We try to keep up to the minute and our interests become momentary. We have so many beautiful houses and an unprecedented number of broken homes. We have accelerated our traveling speed and lost our sense of direction. We have confused running after pleasure with the pursuit of happiness. We have added knowledge without increasing wisdom. We have overstuffed our bodies and starved our souls. We have been so concerned with making a living, we have paid little heed to making a life. We have made of the means of living, the goal of life.

A wealthy retired businessman on a pleasure trip in New Mexico, came upon an able-bodied Indian who was loafing idly during a working day. Our ambitious enterprising businessman was offended by such conspicuous inaction. Turning to the Indian he challenged him: "Why don't you try to get yourself a job?" "Why?" asked the Indian. "Well," said the other, "you could earn as much as $50.00 a week." "Why?" asked the Indian again. "Then you could earn a sum of money and even put some away in the bank." Once again the Indian asked simply, "Why?" "Well," continued the retired friend, "When you saved up enough money you could do as I did. You could retire and you would not have to work anymore." To this the Indian replied: "But I am not working now. Why should I go through all that trouble?"

The Indian's logic was unassailable. If all he would get out of his life's tasks was the ability ultimately to leave them, he had just as well not begin. Our society is filled with people who are making lush livings and lean lives. Are we among them?

Dear friends, Rosh Hashanah not only focuses attention upon these common errors of judgment, it also points to a pattern for eliminating them. "Through penitence, prayer and charity we eliminate our wrong verdicts, our misguided judgments." To our fellow man we should show *Tsdakah*, charity. In the words of the poet Wordsworth, we must learn:

What need there is to be reserved in speech
And temper all our thoughts with charity.

For ourselves we need *T'filah*—which, while it is translated as "prayer," is derived in Hebrew from the root which means, "To judge oneself." That is the true function of prayer at its highest, self-judgment. We must judge ourselves honestly. We must tear away the cloak of rationalization, the mask of pretense so that we can truly conquer our weaknesses.

For life we need *T'shuvah*, literally—"a returning" to a higher conception of life, the kind of life worth praying for. "Remember us to the kind of life which Thou O King desirest."

In judging life let us understand that:

Much as we need something to live with, we need even more, something to live for;

If our lives are not to become spiritual dust-bowls we need regular replenishment from the waters of study, reverence and unselfishness;

Happiness resides not in things but in ourselves;

There is no security like the untroubled conscience;

There is no adventure as exciting as the adventure of a mind and soul which never stop growing;

There is no better exercise for the spirit than bending down to help lift someone up;

The greatest endowment we give our children, is the example of an upright life;

The best portion of a good man's life are, as the poet said, "his little nameless unremembered acts of kindness and of love."

If this be our judgment of life, then our faith need not come in moments. It can be the steady quality of a life which will merit the blessings of the Divine Judge.

MINDING OTHER PEOPLE'S BUSINESS

A research team in London asked people they interviewed what they thought was the most important thing in the world. They came back with the answer: "Minding your own business." This may be true, but on the other hand. . . .

Preached on Shabbat Sh'mot, 1964

12

Minding Other People's Business

SOMEONE has observed, half humorously, half complainingly, that plastic surgeons can do almost anything with a nose except keep it out of other people's business. The ability to mind one's business is a mandatory social virtue. The neighbor who wishes to preserve the neighborly feeling, the mother-in-law who expects to find the warm welcome mat waiting for her on her next visit—indeed, each of us, at the point where our lives intersect the lives of others, must cultivate the fine art of minding our own business. We must learn to draw the delicate distinction between sympathetic, friendly interest which brings people closer, and unsolicited prying and uninvited meddling which puts an intolerable strain on the finest of relationships. The fine art of minding one's own business constitutes one of the required courses in the university of life.

And yet, one of the hallmarks of maturity is the ability to widen the circle of our active concern to the point where it embraces not only our own immediate business, but also the business of other people. This I take it is the meaning of Aristotle's measuring-rod to determine the stature of a man. "If a man is interested in himself only, he is very small; if he is interested in his family he is larger; if he is interested in his community he is larger still." Aristotle is saying, in other words, that the bigger the man, the less likely is he to mind only his own business.

Let us see how forcefully this truth applies to our foremost biblical hero—the man Moses. He seems to have been able to do

137

almost anything except mind his own business. During his most impressionable years he was weaned by his own mother who was engaged by Pharaoh's daughter for that purpose. We can only assume that his mother taught the child his true identity, a grandson of Abraham, Isaac and Jacob.

The time inevitably comes when Moses must be returned to the palace of the Pharaoh. "She brought him unto Pharaoh's daughter and he became her son." It was she who had called him Moses. It was through her that Moses enjoyed all sorts of privileges. Wealth, security, position were all his. Compared to the ordinary Egyptian, he had a most preferred status. Compared to the lot of his fellow Israelites, Moses was not in a palace but in heaven.

There was plenty going on in the palace too. There were banquets, royal visits, magicians, dancers, entertainment and diversions of all sorts. What an opportunity for a Hebrew child whose mother had to conceal him at birth to keep him from being murdered by a royal decree aimed indiscriminately against all Hebrew male infants. This is the stuff that dreams are made of!

But you see, Moses had one special vice that kept him from enjoying all the royal splendor. He simply couldn't mind his own business.

He heard the royal decrees aimed at the Hebrew slaves. He may have seen the plans for the next project to which the slaves were being assigned. He surely heard their groanings and saw the lash marks left by the taskmaster's whip. And all his security in the palace vanished. His wealth dissolved, his privileges turned into torments. Somehow the conviction seized hold of Moses that his brethren's business was his business too.

This is the way the Bible tells it in one cryptic verse: "And it came to pass in those days when Moses was grown up that he went out unto his brethren and looked on their burdens." The die is cast. He is beginning to look at dangerous sights—human burdens. And when a man begins to look upon the burdens of humanity, he begins to understand that he's in a bigger business than he ever imagined existed.

The first day's inspection tour was scarcely a dull one. He hadn't gone very far when "he saw an Egyptian smiting a Hebrew, one of his brethren." Those last words are a crucial phrase. The victim was not simply a Hebrew, another nameless slave. In that slave, Moses saw a piece of himself—"one of his brethren." Caution and prudence probably whispered to Moses: "Moses, look away. Mind your own business." But Moses wasn't listening to the voice of caution. "And he looked this and that way and when he saw there was no man (no one to stand by the Hebrew slave) he smote the Egyptian and hid him in the sand." Not minding his own business is becoming a dangerous way to live.

The second day also has its excitement. Now an incident involves two Hebrews engaged in a quarrel. Apparently, the fact that they are the victims of violent brutality, tends in some measure to brutalize the Hebrew slaves too. For Moses, however, injustice is injustice even when perpetrated by a Hebrew. And so Moses approaches the aggressor and asks him: "Wherefore smitest thou thy brother?" And the other fellow answers: "Who made thee a ruler and a judge over us?" That was the biblical way of saying: "Mind your own business." And the impertinent aggressor goes on to ask rhetorically: "Thinkest thou to kill me as thou didst kill the Egyptian?"

This taunt taught Moses two quick lessons.

1. He was not to expect gratitude for his passionate sense of justice. Minding other people's business can be expensive.
2. The knowledge of his crime was now public.

Soon he learns that Pharaoh is determined to kill him. Imagine! Killing an Egyptian, a member of the master-race, for the innocent pastime of flogging a piece of Hebrew property. And Pharaoh's indignation might very well have been tinged with crimson shame. "Moses! Of all people! After all I did for him! All the education of the palace wasted! All that training gone down the Nile!"

So Moses runs away from Egypt and "dwelt in the land of Midian; and he sat down by a well." It was a nice quiet place to contemplate the high price of minding other people's business. Here was the ideal spot for a rest cure—to repent of his foolishness.

But his quiet is soon disturbed. The narrative continues: "Now the priest of Midian had seven daughters; and they came and drew water and filled the troughs to water their father's flock. And the shepherds came and drove them away; but Moses stood up and helped them and watered their flock."

Poor Moses! When will he ever learn? This time there were no Hebrews involved, no brethren. These young ladies were total strangers. But that's how it is with a man who cannot mind his own business. He soon loses the ability to discriminate between one of his brethren and Midianites. Injustice is injustice regardless of the color of the victim's skin or the nature of his creed.

Well, while this has been going on, Pharaoh may have become enraged, some Hebrews suspicious, and the Midianite shepherds affronted by the gall of this stranger. But God has been watching approvingly. God likes a man who looks after the defenseless and the down-trodden. And from the burning bush God gives Moses one of the biggest pieces of somebody else's business to mind that any human being ever received.

Go back to Egypt, Moses. Confront the Pharaoh who wants to kill you. Talk to the Hebrews about freedom. Neither the Pharaoh nor the Israelites will take kindly to you, Moses. But from now on their business is your business.

From this point on, the history is well known. It is interesting to speculate, however, about what would have happened if Moses had indeed minded his own business, if he had embraced the palace and all it stood for. Of course we shall never know, but at least this much we can say for certain. We would not be talking about Moses today because he would have no claim upon our memory. And, most assuredly, the intervening history of men would have been decisively different.

Henrich Heine did not overstate the case when he said: "Since the days of Moses, justice speaks with a Hebrew accent." On Jewish history, Moses' imprint has been even larger. He created the classic spiritual profile of the ideal Jewish personality—the prophet. He is not a recluse who withdraws from an unregenerate society to carve out his own salvation in splendid but selfish isolation. He cannot separate himself from the very community which he condemns so thoroughly. He must go out to his brethren, descend into the market-place and be prepared to get battered and bruised in the encounter. All this he does because he knows that the business of his fellow-man is his business too. In reality, it is not that he cannot mind his own business but that he has an enlarged sense of what his own business is.

It is out of this enlarged conception of the area of the prophet's vital concern that there are born such questions as: "Have we not all one father? Hath not one God created us all? Why then do we deal treacherously each man against his neighbor?" It is out of this expanded awareness of the extent of his own business that the prophet Isaiah who hears God ask: "Whom shall I send?" must respond: "Here I am, send me!"

This is one of our truly decisive contributions to man's spiritual quest. It is a note which has been sounded whenever men have been able to see themselves in the larger human perspective.

When Solon was asked how justice could be secured in Athens, he answered: "If those who are not injured feel as indignant as those who are."

Theodore Roosevelt was making the same point when he declared: "This country will not be a good place for any of us to live in unless we make it a good place for all of us to live in." True as this observation is, we realize today that it does not go far enough. Substitute "world" for "country" and we get much closer to the heart of the matter. A Sputnick which circles the globe in something like ninety-six minutes drives home the inescapable truth that the world has been shrunk more than an inexpensive shirt in the hands of a careless laundryman. A diplomatic epigram of a generation ago announced that if France sneezes all of Europe catches cold. Today we realize that if any nation, however small, gets sick, the fever shoots through the body of all nations. Slowly, painfully and at an exorbitant cost, this truth has been insinuating itself into the reluctant minds of statesmen. The United Nations is a living symbol of the collective consent of humanity to the principle by which Moses ordered his life—no man can afford to mind only his own business.

This matter does not only concern relations between nations. It comes right into our neighborhoods and the street we live on. It talks to us about small, everyday affairs. It tells us that those who fail to develop the sympathetic imagination necessary to become involved in other people's business miss some of life's most abiding satisfactions:

> She built herself a little house
> All walled about with Pride;
> Took Prudence as a servant,
> And locked herself inside.
>
> She drew the blinds down tight as tight
> When Sorrow chanced to roam.
> Experience called—she sent down word
> That she was not at home.
>
> Then wherefore should she now complain
> And wherefore should she sigh,
> That Life and Love and Laughter
> Have passed unseeing by?

Life is more rewarding and made more livable by people who have the compassion to become concerned with the sorrows of others, their illnesses, their needs, their aches, their troubles. These people are the solid nails that keep the world together.

The late Ernie Pyle gave us a glimpse into the difference a person like that makes. "When my mother suffered a stroke of paralysis, Anny Kearns, one of our neighbors, didn't say: 'Now if there's anything at all that I can do. . . .' She said: 'Mary, I'll be there at 7:30 in the morning to do the washing for you!' And she was too."

One of the most beautiful rabbinic lessons which was incorporated into the daily prayer book was designed to encourage every Jew to develop a magnified sense of his own business. "These are the *mitzvot*," the Mishna taught, "whose fruit a man enjoys in this world while the principal remains for him to all eternity." Among these kind deeds of inexhaustible blessing are included: performing deeds of loving-kindness, hospitality to way-farers, visiting the sick, and making peace between a man and his fellowman. Here are the traditional Jewish dimensions of the extent of your own business and mine which we are committed to mind.

A business block in one of our western cities displays this motto: "Service is the rent we pay for the space we occupy." As human beings, dedicated service to one another is the rent we pay for the space we occupy on God's earth.

THE NEED OF A PRESENCE

A line from one of George Eliot's poems reminds us of the powerful influence exerted upon us by the things we carry within us. In this sermon specific attention is focused upon three vital forces that can mold our lives.

Preached on Yom Kippur, 1961

THE NEED OF A RULER

13

The Need of a Presence

IN ONE of her best known poems, "The Choir Invisible,"
George Eliot reveals some sentiments which are at the very
heart of this Yizkor hour.

> Oh, may I join the choir invisible
> Of those immortal dead who live again
> In minds made better by their presence; live
> In pulses stirred to generosity,
> In deeds of daring rectitude, in scorn
> For miserable aims that end with self,
> In thoughts sublime that pierce the night like stars,
> And with their mild persistence urge men's search
> To vaster issues.

She speaks of "those immortal dead who live again in
minds. . . ." This is an echo of sound Jewish teaching. It is not
only God who keeps "His faith with those who sleep in the dust."
We, too, can and should do so. When the dead live again in our
minds, as they do during this Yizkor hour, we invest them with
immortality, with deathlessness.

But George Eliot goes further. She speaks "of those immortal
dead who live again in minds made better by their presence." Here
she suggests a second theme of the Yizkor hour. By remembering
the dead we confer immortality upon them and they in turn re-
ciprocate our kindness by ennobling our lives. "In minds made
better by their presence."

This morning I should like to consider with you the truth that among our greatest needs for vital and creative living is the need of a presence. And I should like to suggest further that there are three types of presence that we need.

The first is the presence within us of an inspiring example, a model worthy of our emulation.

The biblical story of Joseph is one of the most stirring success stories ever told. It traces the most meteoric career in the Bible as a slave boy moves from the depths of the pit to virtually a monarch's throne. The greater drama however is not in the outward achievements but in the inner growth and development of Joseph. One of his truly noteworthy triumphs comes when he is tempted to betray his master Potiphar by yielding to the advances of his wife. Joseph, as we know, resists that temptation Our sages, in trying to account for Joseph's moral strength, attribute it to "his father's image," which appeared to him in his moment of testing and gave him the strength to resist. Joseph took with him the presence of Jacob.

All of us need the presence of moral and spiritual heroes. The measure of our own achievements is often a reflection of the size of the heroes we have chosen to emulate.

One of the great indictments against the screen and television is the kind of heroes it holds up for our children to emulate. The models are shabby and unworthy of emulation. How many of the people who flit across the screens can serve as the presence we want our children to carry with them, to give them inspiration and strength, to overcome their weakness, to elicit their best, to put highest priority of things of the spirit. There are many reasons why we urge a Jewish education but surely not the least of these is that in our heroes' gallery are men and women whose lives can inspire our children to reach upward and outward.

"Success," said H. G. Wells, "is to be measured not by wealth, power or fame but by the ratio between what a man is and what he might be." In order to become what we might be, to realize our full stature as human beings, we need desperately to carry within ourselves the challenging and uplifting presence of a noble model. Maurice Samuel, one of our most gifted authors and surely the most prolific writer on the American-Jewish scene, has dedicated the better portion of his time and creative energies to the service of his people. In one of his personal revelations he speaks of the profound role Chaim Weizmann has played in his life. He calls him "the central figure in my dominating life interest. Though I shall perhaps survive him by a few years, my usefulness, such as it is, will continue to derive from the days of my discipleship. His spiritual craftsmanship is written into many lives, of which mine is one."

Lewis Carroll, the author of *Alice In Wonderland*, once wrote a little fantasy involving a clock that kept crying in distress: "I'm looking for someone to unlock me." Like so many of Carroll's writings this one, too, speaks of real human problems. We each need someone to unlock us, to release our creative powers, to tap our wells of kindness and sympathy, to urge us to search for "vaster issues."

For some of us, our own beloved dead are the keys which can unlock us. For others it is the tall spirits of our Jewish past. For some it is the benefactors of humanity of whom we have read and with whom we identify. For some of us it is our husbands or our wives or even our children who bring out the best within us, who give us strength to remain true and pure. For some it is all of these together in some measure. For surely no life can be truly unlocked without the presence of an inspiring example.

In addition to the presence of an inspiring example, we need the presence of an inspiring ideal. The name of Louis Pasteur is revered today wherever "pasteurized" milk is served. In France a few years ago, the school children voted him as the Frenchman who had done the most for their country in its entire history. But in his time, Pasteur had to fight a bitter and lonely struggle against all kinds of professional pride and jealousy. When he was at last elected to the coveted membership in the French Academy, he indicated to the hushed audience in his inaugural address how he had persevered in spite of the enormous obstacles he had to hurdle on the road to victory. "Blessed is he who carries within himself an ideal and who obeys it; an ideal of art or of science or of religious virtues. Therein lie the springs of great thoughts and great actions."

We, no less than Pasteur, need the shiny presence of an ideal which we must each carry within if obstacles are not to defeat us, if life is not to corrupt us, if our values are not to forsake us. These days are not particularly congenial to ideals. The spirit of cynicism nibbles away at them from all sides. Words like self-dedication, self-sacrifice, self-discipline are not prominent in the contemporary American vocabulary. And they are not prominent in our vocabulary because they are inconspicuous in our thinking. Today, if we want to discredit a proposal, we call it idealistic. If we want to undermine a person, we label him an idealist. And yet is there any greater compliment when you pause to think of it, than to be a true idealist, to remain constant, unwavering, uncompromised in our loyalty to the best we know? Is it not true that unless we truly stand for something, we have fallen in our human stature? If we do not harbor within us something which is above us, wherein is our eminence over the animals below us? We desperately need the presence of an ideal to give life its distinction and its glory, to do for us what Zionism did for Theodor Herzl. "Zionism," he wrote, "was the Sabbath of my life."

It is told of a great artist that he always kept a number of beautiful gems on his easel; sapphire, emerald and ruby. When asked the reason, he said that there was a danger of his colors being faded by usage and his eye getting toned down so that the tints would lose their brilliance. So he kept his eye toned up by constantly referring to these original colors that could not fade.

Here again Judaism serves us well. There are many reasons for coming regularly to worship in the synagogue. One of the most vital reasons is to look regularly at the original colors, to keep our eyes from becoming toned down, to remind ourselves of the values and ideals which give life beauty and meaning. In brief, to renew within us the presence of our ideals.

For last, I have left the most important presence which we need—the presence of God. "I have set the Lord before me always." We need that Presence when like Jacob we face the unknown and the uncharted tomorrow. Living as we do in a world of ominous, atomic rumblings, we too need to hear the reassuring words God spoke to Jacob on his way to Egypt. "Fear not to go down into Egypt. . . . I will go down into Egypt with you and I will go up with you again."

"Wherever the Israelites wandered, the Divine Presence wandered with them." We Jews took God with us into exile. We were oft forsaken and declared outcasts by men, but we were never alone. We carried that Presence with us into all the far-flung lands of our dispersion. We need that Presence today.

We need the presence of God when we lie in a sick bed. Finding ourselves in a hospital room is often a frightening and revolutionary experience. Previously we were busy, occupied, doing things. Now we are not movers, we are moved. We are not doers, we are passive. Apprehensively we hang upon the doctor's verdict. Our privacy is invaded. Our weakness is emphasized. Our dependence is magnified. Our fears are given free play.

Edith Hamilton, writing on Greek tragedy, makes this relevant statement: "Pain is the most individualizing thing on earth. It is true that it is the great common bond as well, but that realization comes only when it is over. To suffer is to be alone; to watch another suffer is to know the barrier that shuts each of us away by himself." In the aloneness of a hospital room we need the

151

comforting Presence to reassure us, to abide with us through the long dark night.

We need a presence when we are overcome with bereavement. "The heart knows its own bitterness and no stranger shares its joy." We try to share in one another's sorrow. We perform small courtesies, soft acts of compassion. But in the heart of the mourner there is an emptiness that friends cannot fill; which can be filled only by the presence of God. "Yea though I walk through the valley of the shadow of death, I fear no evil for Thou art with me."

After he lost someone very dear to him one man said to his friend: "You who stand in the sunshine may believe in God but I who stand in the shadow must believe in Him. I have nothing else."

We need a presence when life is kind, when we prosper and taste the heady wine of success, when we are sorely tempted to that greatest of all idolatries—self-deification.

We need the presence of God as we grow older, when we have said many a goodbye to a loved one, when the friends on the other side far outnumber those on this side, as the thought of death, our death, closes in on us. The thought frightens us but if we have the Presence with us, should we be? Perhaps if we had possessed consciousness we would have been afraid of being born, of surrendering that secure and comfortable prenatal world for the unknown world outside. But the world into which we were born was ready to look after our needs. There were loving arms to enfold us, open hearts to admit us, soft lips to kiss us. Will God, who provided all things for us at the entrance desert us at the exit? Does He not know how much we are still children who frighten easily, and will He not be there to see that we are not left alone in our new surroundings? Can we really travel beyond the range of His care and His concern? Is there any place devoid of His presence? Holy, holy, holy is the Lord of hosts. The whole universe is filled with His glory.

G. K. Chesterton once said that if he were drowning he would rather meet a burglar who could swim than a bishop who couldn't. That may be true. But there are ever so many crises in life where help comes not from without but from within. There are the deep waters from which not even a swimming bishop could save us, no one except our own resources of spirit and soul and heart. There are times, in brief, when we are strong as the Presence we carry within us.

At *Yizkor* time, our thoughts would not be complete if we did not add an important corollary to our theme. We not only need a presence, we *become* a presence. Every moment of every day of our lives we are entering into the lives of others.

> His little arms crept 'round my neck
> And then I heard him say
> Four simple words I shan't forget,
> Four words that made me pray. . . .
>
> They turned a mirror on my soul,
> On secrets no one knew.
> They startled me, I hear them yet;
> He said "I'll be like you!"

While the impress is strongest upon those who are nearest to us, upon our children, our mates, brothers, sisters, neighbors, clients, customers, patients—it is not confined to these. Our influence is as wide as the radius of our lives.

What kind of a presence am I now? What kind of a presence shall I remain in the time to come? What will others recall of my life? George Eliot herself must have asked herself these questions, because she expressed the hope which can well be the central prayer of our lives.

> May I reach
> That purest heaven,—be to other souls

FINDING OURSELVES

The cup of strength in some great agony,
Enkindle generous ardor, feed pure love,
Beget the smiles that have no cruelty,
Be the sweet presence of a good diffused,
And in diffusion ever more intense!
So shall I join the choir invisible
Whose music is the gladness of the world.

OVERLOOKING THE OBVIOUS

An admonition from a well-known detective in the world of fiction has genuine significance for us in the world of reality. It calls attention to a common human failing which prevents us from seeing so many vital things which we can overlook only to our own deep impoverishment. It reminds us to open our eyes and see.

Preached on Rosh Hashanah, 1958

14

Overlooking the Obvious

ON RARE occasions, when I turn to reading mystery stories I do so for relaxation not for inspiration. Imagine my surprised delight therefore when one such story recently yielded a thought so compelling that I resolved to share it with you, my friends, on this exalted day when we are gathered to appraise our past, to chart our future.

Hercule Poirot, the detective hero of Agatha Christie's tales, says to his good friend Captain Hastings: "It is your destiny to stand beside me and prevent me from committing the unforgivable error."

"What do you call the unforgivable error?" the captain asks. And the detective answers: "Overlooking the obvious."

I have chosen this theme for our consideration because I believe that the tendency to overlook the obvious is one of our most widespread human shortcomings.

This tendency has been enormously accentuated by the breathtaking scientific breakthroughs achieved during the last twelve months. We have penetrated outer space with man-made satellites. The atomic submarine, the Nautilus, carried man for the first time under the Arctic ice cap across the top of the world under water. The next radio announcement may tell of a successful rocket thrust to or around the moon. "Reaching for the moon," is no longer a metaphor of futility. It is an item on the scientist's agenda. Manned flights to our nearest neighbors in the solar system: the moon, Mars and Venus, are being confidently expected within the coming decade. Taken together, these staggering forward thrusts of the human intellect have understandably helped focus our attention on distant horizons and far-away places. More than ever before, we who live during these days of vanishing barriers and crumbling frontiers of space are prone to commit the "unforgivable error" of overlooking the crucial matters so close at hand. And it is precisely the familiar, immediate, commonplace areas of life that we must explore if we are to live abundantly, zestfully and purposefully.

To illustrate this truth, let us consider three biblical personalities, each of them in a climactic experience of their lives, each of them dramatizing another aspect of our impoverishing habit of overlooking the obvious, each of them able to help prevent us from committing the unforgivable error.

The first is Hagar, Abraham's Egyptian servant, of whom we read in the Torah selection earlier this morning. We find her and her son Ishmael dying of thirst in the wilderness of Beer-sheba. Despairingly, she places her child under one of the shrubs and removes herself at some distance. "For she said: 'Let me not look upon the death of the child.' . . . And God opened her eyes and she saw a well of water; and she went and filled the bottle with water, and gave the lad drink."

Let us note carefully what the Torah tells us about Hagar's deliverance. God did not create a well in answer to her desperate prayers. The well had been there all along. Her source of salvation and survival was close at hand. What God did for Hagar was to open her eyes so that she saw the well, the obvious she had overlooked.

How I wish that God would do for us what He did for Hagar —simply open our eyes to the unnumbered glories that surround us, the extravagant beauty that enfolds us, the manifold blessings which sustain us. If only we could see the obvious, what an effective antidote that would be to our gnawing discontent, our insatiable ambitions, our quiet desperation, our restless nights, our parched days. God has placed us in a Garden of Eden and instead of feeding upon its varied delights, we are forever drawn to the apple He placed off limits. So preoccupied are we with what we lack that we are unmindful of what we possess. A well-known English author and critic reminded us of this when he wrote: "I am not surprised at what men suffer but I am surprised at what men miss."

The newspapers recently carried a touching story of a mother who was taking her little son to Salt Lake City on a melancholy mission. The boy had lost the sight of one eye several years previous and in the intervening years, medical men had tried valiantly to save his remaining eye. Now they had come to the reluctant conclusion that the eye could not be saved. Before the darkness set in, his mother wanted the boy to have a fond lingering look at the majestic mountains of Utah so that he could take that splendid image with him into the sightless future. Can we read such a story without becoming acutely aware of the myriad marvels which constantly beckon to us and which we persistently overlook precisely because they are so many and so obvious?

Helen Keller is most sensitive to this common failing and there is a special poignancy to the words she wrote in *The World I Live In.* "I have walked with people whose eyes are full of light but who see nothing in woods, sea or sky, nothing in the city street, nothing in books. What a witless masquerade is this seeing.

"It were better far to sail forever in the night of blindness with sense and feeling and mind than to be thus content with the mere act of seeing.

"They have the sunset, the morning skies, the purple of distant hills, yet their souls voyage through this enchanted world with nothing but a barren stare."

As we grow older our eyesight usually grows weaker and when we finally summon up the courage to admit it publicly we head for the oculist to restore our eyes to their maximum efficiency.

Another hazard of growing older is that our capacity to look at things with wonder and enthusiasm also grows weaker. There was a time when a sunset brought to mind the poet's description of "the skies yet blushing with departing light." Now we see the sunset and murmur: "I'd better hurry or I'll be late for dinner." The first snow of winter used to fill us with wild anticipation of adventures exhilarating, daring and mischievous. Now we start worrying about who is going to do the shoveling. The prospect of wearing a new pair of shoes to school for the first time, used to be enough to arouse us two hours before our normal waking hour. Today, we buy a $3,500 automobile and when a friend asks us, "What's new?" we say: "Nothing." "There was a time," H. G. Wells wrote in the twilight of his life, "when my little soul shone and was uplifted at the starry enigma of the sky. That has gone absolutely. Now I can go out and look at the stars as I look at the pattern of wallpaper on a railway station waiting room." Are there any eyeglasses to correct this variety of defective sight? Should we not therefore pray that God will do for us what He did for Hagar: open our eyes in the wilderness so that we see the wells of beauty and inspiration that surround us on all sides?

> "Earth's crammed with heaven
> And every common bush afire with God;
> But only he who sees, takes off his shoes,
> The rest sit round it and pluck blackberries."

This verse by Elizabeth Barrett Browning which suggests that we see not only the beauty of nature but also the artist who fashioned it leads us to a second aspect of our theme, which emerges out of a decisive experience in the life of Jacob.

Jacob is fleeing the wrath of his brother Esau who has vowed to kill him. Nightfall finds him tired, frightened and alone, quite remote from any outpost of civilization. He makes his bed on the cold earth, using stones for his pillow. And in his sleep he has the well-known dream of the ladder that scrapes heaven, the angels who ascend and descend upon it, and a wondrous vision of God who assures him: "Behold, I am with thee and will keep thee wherever thou goest." Then the Torah adds this revealing sequence: "And Jacob awoke out of his sleep, and he said: 'Surely the Lord is in this place and I knew it not.' And he was afraid and said: 'How full of awe is this place! This is none other than the house of God and this is the gate of heaven.' "

Now this was a remarkable admission for Jacob to make. He had from his earliest childhood absorbed a belief in God—the God who revealed Himself to his grandfather Abraham and to his father Isaac. It was in the name of that God, that Isaac had in fact blessed him before his hasty departure from his home. But Jacob now confesses that his conception of God had been limited by geographical boundaries. When he was in his own birthplace, he was under the jurisdiction and within the domain of God. As soon as he left the city, he believed that he had left his God behind. He had gone beyond the sphere of His influence. It took the splendid vision to teach him: "Behold the Lord is in this place and I knew it not." In the darkness of night, God opened Jacob's eyes to the obvious truth he had overlooked that God, by definition, must be everywhere if He is anywhere.

The centuries that separate us from Jacob have witnessed a refinement and an expansion of our concept of God. Today, even the most unsophisticated believing Jew would not be guilty of the kind of naivete that Jacob displayed. In our prayers we repeat Isaiah's impassioned outburst: *Kadosh, kadosh, kadosh Adonoi tzavaot, m'lo kol ha-aretz kavodo,* "Holy, Holy, Holy is the Lord of hosts, the whole earth is full of His glory." One of the names by which we designate God in Hebrew is "Makom," which means "place" by way of illustrating our belief, as the philosopher Saadia put it, that "there is no place devoid of Him." A finite God, a limited God, is a contradiction in terms.

And yet I often have occasion to wonder how fervently we accept with our hearts and minds what we affirm with our lips concerning the omnipresence of God. Do our actions in our offices and places of business harmonize with a belief that God is present at every transaction and listens to every conversation? Are we prepared to submit our ledgers to His scrutiny? Does our treatment of our subordinates reflect the kind of humility that comes from knowing "before whom thou standest," or do we in fact so lord it over others as to convey the blasphemous impression that we are God? How many of us are prepared to follow the motto one shoe manufacturer adopted for himself: "God first, others second, shoes third?" When we succeed in our ventures or prosper in our undertakings, do we attribute the results to our merits or to His mercies? When sorrow lays its heavy hand upon us or illness saps our strength and drains our hopes, do we feel alone and forsaken or do we hold firm to the faith of the Psalmist: "The Lord is nigh unto them that are of a broken heart"? After these Holy Days are over will we bid farewell to God or will we invite Him along with us throughout the days to come? Will we comport ourselves in our homes, our factories, our offices, our places of amusement, our Jewish organizations in such a way as to bear testimony that we do indeed believe: "This is none other than the house of God and this is the gate of heaven"?

Many of us, I am sure, are familiar with the Yiddish folksong called "A Dudele." It is an affectionate salute to God who is addressed as "Du"—the intimate form of "you" in Yiddish. The song asks—"Where can I find You?" and in true Yiddish style it answers the question by asking another—"Where can't I find You?" In prosperity and adversity—You. East—You. West—You. North—You. South—You. Heaven—You. Earth—You. Where I turn and where I go—only You.

These are the Jewish dimensions of God. Are they the dimensions of the God we ourselves believe in or are we still overlooking the obvious truth God taught Jacob: "Behold the Lord is in this place?"

The third and last biblical figure whose eyes God opened to a vital and obvious truth was the heathen prophet Balaam. Balaam, we may recall, was engaged by Balak, the King of Moab, to pronounce a curse upon the ancient Israelites who were approaching his country en route to their promised land. Balak had heard of their military victories over other peoples and feared that his people would also prove powerless against them. (Had he checked the reports more carefully, he would have learned that the Israelites had waged battle only when it was thrust upon them. But that is another matter.) So Balak offered Balaam an impressive fee to practice his celebrated skill of invoking doom upon these approaching hordes. But Balak was destined for a shock. After Balaam had gone through all his incantations and preparations, he who had come to curse remained to bless. And in some of the most lyrical poetry in the Torah, Balaam extols the praises of the Israelites. Among his words of lavish tribute is the well-known verse with which we begin our services. "How goodly are thy tents O Jacob, thy dwelling places O Israel." Significantly, Balaam says of himself at the start of his peroration: "Thus sayeth the man whose eyes have been opened."

As I look out upon the contemporary Jewish scene I cannot resist the prayer that the eyes of some of our fellow-Jews might similarly be opened so that they too might see the goodliness of the tents of Jacob. So often when a "Jewish" novel appears by a Jewish writer I begin to read it with trepidation and usually my worst fears are realized. What emerges is too frequently not a picture of Jewish life but a caricature, and in so far as these books mirror anything at all, they only reveal the nakedness and the self-hatred of their authors.

The most recent calumny against the Jews is to be found in *The Enemy Camp*, by Jerome Weidman. This is neither the time nor the occasion to go into this book in detail. But I would like to call attention to one unfortunate statement which appears at the very end of the book and is evidently designed to constitute the author's message. Our hero is recalling what Uncle Zisha told him: "Do what your heart tells you, not your religion. It's more important to be a man than a Jew, Uncle Zisha had said, and without listening to your heart you'll never be a man."

So! Is that the choice that confronts you and me—to be a man or to be a Jew? Is there indeed a conflict between the two or is it not truer by far that I am most the man when I am most the Jew? Is there any more noble path to manhood that the road of Jewish living which includes such sign posts as "Thou shalt love thy neighbor as thyself," "Ye shall be holy for I the Lord your God am holy," "Justice, justice shalt thou pursue," "Ye shall love the stranger for ye were strangers in the land of Egypt"? Do we become men by ceasing to be Jews?

I pity the Jew who would so besmirch the name of the Jew! May God have mercy on his confused soul.

If he would permit his eyes to be opened he might read the words written in *Awakened*, by Margaret Abrams, herself a convert to Judaism: "To be a Jew is a most splendid way to be a human being." Ludwig Lewisohn, a Jew who strayed and then returned because his eyes were opened, wrote: "To be a Jew is to be a friend of mankind, to be a proclaimer of liberty and peace." If, as I suspect, Mr. Weidman would be more impressed by the words of a non-Jew, I refer him to George Bernard Shaw who said: "The Jew is born civilized." The Christian theologian, Carl Cornill, wrote: "Israel gave the world the sense of true humanity." An American Protestant minister, Henry Edmonds, addressed these words to the Jew: "We have taken your Bible over and made it ours, and said never a word of appreciation of the genius for God which produced it. . . . We have called peace

164

a Christian attitude, forgetting that it was a Jew (Isaiah) who first used these words, which now belong to humanity, about beating swords into ploughshares and spears into pruning hooks."

Yes, brother Weidman, these are some of the value judgments of your people you might have brought to the attention of your fellow Americans. Instead you chose to join the enemy camp, the detractors and vilifiers of a much maligned and abused people.

But is it fair to direct all our shafts against one man without reserving a healthy measure of criticism for ourselves for spawning such writers? If they who presume to speak on our behalf have not had their eyes opened to the beauty and the nobility of the tents of Jacob, is it not in appreciable measure the consequence of our own failure to discover that beauty for ourselves. If our sons and daughters turn novelists, what manner of images and impressions will they convey of what transpires within the dwelling-places of Israel? What kind of memories are we fashioning? Are they filled with warmth, with understanding, with dedication, with a sense of commitment? Do we not owe our children, our ancestors, as well as ourselves, a more intimate acquaintance with that which is uniquely ours so that our lives may be richer and the chain of the generations uncorroded? Are we not duty bound to have our own eyes opened?

John Ruskin once wrote: "The greatest thing a human soul ever does in this world is to see something. Hundreds of people can talk to one who can think, but thousands can think for one who can see. To see clearly is poetry, philosophy and religion all in one."

On Rosh Hashanah we ask God for so much. When it comes to making demands upon Him, we are not bashful. Perhaps if we were wise, we should ask Him not to grant us one more gift until we have learned to see what is already ours. In our morning prayers we praise God who is the *Pokayach Ivrim,* the opener of the eyes of the blind. Sight we have, thank God. Now we must pray for insight.

May God grant us all on the New Year the capacity to see the obvious we so frequently overlook.

May He open our eyes to the beauty and the loveliness of the world in which He has placed us.

May He open our eyes to His presence at all times and in every circumstance.

May He open our eyes to the glory of our heritage.

For in truth, "to see clearly is poetry, philosophy and religion all in one."

PARADOXES OF HAPPINESS

The framers of our Declaration of Independence included the pursuit of happiness among man's "unalienable rights." It has even been one of his major preoccupations. But is happiness to be pursued? Where is it to be found? The answers take the form of three paradoxes.

Preached on Rosh Hashanah, 1959

15

Paradoxes of Happiness

THE HIGH HOLY DAY liturgy is saturated with prayers of extraordinary beauty. One of the most touching of these is the prayer found in the Amidah. "Remember us unto life, O King who delightest in life; inscribe us in the book of life for Thy sake O King of life."

This is the articulation of our deepest yearning. It flows naturally from the human heart. *Es vill zich leben,* "We want to live." The world is beautiful and it is good to be alive. As we grow older I think we are less inclined to take life for granted. Every year finds our list of comrades and loved ones a little more diminished. Inevitably on Rosh Hashanah we remember those who answered the final summons since last Rosh Hashanah. These reflections sadden us but they also deepen our gratitude for the elementary blessing of life. As we become more mindful of our human frailty an added sense of urgency creeps into our voices when we pray "Remember us unto life, O King who delightest in life." We are in love with life.

But even as we ask for continued life, a haunting question lurks in the background. Are we willing to accept life on any terms? Infinitely precious though life is, are there not conditions which would make life too burdensome, too intolerable? Is mere biological survival enough?

No, we want more than another year of life. As our Rosh Hashanah greetings indicate, we wish each other a happy New Year. We are praying for a happy life. But what is happiness? What can we ourselves do to achieve it? I do not believe that

169

God can give us happiness. God can give us many blessings but whether they bring happiness depends very largely upon us. Happiness is not a gift, it is an achievement.

Before we try to discover what happiness is and how it may be achieved, let us briefly indicate what happiness is not, and where we ought not to seek it.

Despite the exaggerated and distorted emphasis in our lives upon the feverish competition to acquire things—more things, bigger things, better things—happiness is not found in things. If it were, all the rich would be happy. And incidentally, compared to the rest of the world, almost any American is a plutocrat. Once we go beyond providing for our basic needs, possessions can only add to our physical comfort and there is a vast difference between being comfortable and being happy.

Nor is it found in artificially stimulated merry-making. Some of the saddest sights are those who are forever chasing pleasures. Happiness does not come in liquid form. There is a world of difference between forgetting yourself and fulfilling yourself.

Genuine happiness is not expensive but we often pay exorbitant prices for its imitations.

Nor is it far away. "The foolish man seeks happiness in the distance; the wise grows it under his feet." Indeed Helen Keller who was given such meagre equipment with which to confront life, said "Your success and happiness lie in you." How can we achieve happiness?

I would be less than honest if I were to imply that there is a sure road to happiness, that it is perfectly known to me and that I can put you on it in one easy sermon. None of these is true. But I should like to share with you some of my thoughts on this subject which can perhaps serve as signposts along the road, helping us on our quest.

I would like to sum up my reflections in three paradoxes. The first is this. If we seek happiness, it will elude us. We find it only when we are not looking for it.

The American Declaration of Independence is one of the greatest human documents ever written, but it does contain one misleading phrase—"the pursuit of happiness." It gives the impression that happiness must be pursued, and that if pursued it can be caught. Neither is true. Happiness is a by-product, something you achieve while you are altogether intent on doing something else. The moment you start concentrating on happiness, it fades away. The intense pursuit of happiness is one of the chief sources of unhappiness. When we court happiness too intensely, it is frightened away.

This fundamental truth was captured in the parable of the big dog who saw a little dog chasing his tail and asked him, "Why are you chasing your tail?" "Well, said the puppy, "I have been told that the best thing for a dog is happiness and that happiness is in my tail. Therefore I am chasing it. When I catch it, I shall have happiness."

"Listen son," said the big dog, "I too want happiness and I too have been told that it is to be found in my tail. But I noticed that when I chase after it, it keeps running away from me, but when I go about my business, it comes after me."

This is the secret—going about one's business, totally intent on doing a worthwhile task and never running after the tail. When we keep asking ourselves, "Am I happy?" we are no wiser than if we should pause several times during the day to take our temperature to discover whether we are healthy. In the latter case we are more prone to become sick; in the former we are quite likely to grow miserable.

Some years ago a London newspaper offered prizes for the best answers to this question: "Who are the happiest persons on earth?" Here are three of the answers which were judged the best:

1. A craftsman or artist whistling over a job that is well done.
2. A mother after a busy day bathing her baby.
3. A doctor who has finished a difficult and dangerous operation and saved a human life.

Notice that not one of these people is looking for happiness. Each has an important task at hand and is totally absorbed in performing it. And in the act of going about their business, they have unwittingly opened a door by which happiness has quietly entered. You see, happiness enjoys seeing us about our business. She comes to the farmer in his fields, the worker at his lathe, the writer at his desk, the housewife at her mixing bowl. She is attracted by the smell of sweat, by the sight of overalls, by the sound of tools. She tiptoes in so softly we scarcely take note of her presence. She lays her blessings upon us all unawares.

In his book, *How To Be Happy Though Human*, Dr. W. Beran Wolfe summed up this thought in these words: "If you observe a really happy man, you will find him building a boat, writing a symphony, educating his son, growing double dahlias in his garden or looking for dinosaur eggs in the Gobi Desert. He will not be searching for happiness as if it were a collar button that has rolled under the radiator. He will not be striving for it as a goal in itself."

No, happiness cannot be overtaken by those who pursue her. Happiness is a by-product of cheerful, honest labor dedicated to a worthwhile task.

We proceed now to what I consider a second paradox about happiness. You cannot get happiness unless you give it. The truth is suggested by the Hebrew word for life which is *chayim*—a plural noun. In Hebrew there is no singular noun for one life. Any life is a plural noun, as though to drive home the inescapable fact that life to be good cannot be singular. If we would achieve happiness our lives must spill over into other lives. We

PARADOXES OF HAPPINESS

must concentrate not on getting but on giving, not on hoarding but on sharing.

Think back for a moment to the three most popular conceptions of a happy person. Not one is in the act of receiving. They are all going out of themselves. The mother is bringing comfort to her baby, the surgeon has saved the life of another and even the craftsman and the artist have contributed a vital part of themselves, their skill or genius, to the creation of something which others will enjoy using or looking at.

John Mason Brown, the well-known critic, said something extremely relevant on this matter: "What happiness is, no person can say for another. But no one, I am convinced, can be happy who lives only for himself. The joy of living comes from immersion in something that we know to be bigger, better, more enduring and worthier than we are."

How I wish that more of us would grasp the full meaning of these words! If only we accepted the explosive significance with which they are charged. We would not say "no" to causes which beg for volunteers. We would not shut our eyes to human need. We would not be perennial seekers after diversion, recreation and escape from which we return to an inner emptiness which will not be filled by self-pampering.

One of the real danger zones in a woman's life is that very period which she eagerly anticipated when the problem of raising children seemed so burdensome. Oh how delightful life will be when Joey is grown and Sue is a young lady. They will become more self-reliant, they will require less physical care and attention. I'll be free: Then what happens? *Gott helft*, the years go by and freedom has dawned. But sad to relate, the anticipated happiness does not come with freedom. On the contrary, the mother will frequently become more unhappy as the children become more independent. Now she wonders whether she is needed. The children seem so self-sufficient it hurts.

173

If she is wise, she will accept this loosening of the strings as nature's way of preparing the child for responsible adulthood. She will also realize that while she may be less needed physically, her children's dependence upon her for guidance, encouragement and counsel is still exceedingly large. And, most important, if she didn't do so earlier she will begin to search earnestly for an occupation, a cause, or an organization to which she can direct her surplus time and energy. Shortly, the children will leave altogether and her need to give of herself will be even greater. Her happiness depends upon finding a worthy object of her skill, her time and her talents.

What is true of this mother at this particular time is true of all of us at all times. We cannot have happiness unless we give of ourselves. Dr. Albert Schweitzer, one of the truly tall spirits of our time, put the essence of the matter simply: "One thing I know; the only ones among you who will be really happy are those who will have sought and found how to serve."

This is the crucial thing. We make a living by what we get. We make a life by what we give.

The third paradox of happiness flows directly from the second. In fact, it is the second one turned around. If it is true that we cannot get happiness unless we give it, it is also true that we cannot give it without getting it. Happiness has correctly been compared to a perfume. You cannot pour it on others without getting a few drops on yourself.

Few living Americans have enjoyed as many well-deserved honors as has the Negro contralto Marion Anderson. She was selected as America's ambassador of good will to Asia. She was invited to sing in the White House. She won acclaim from some of the musical immortals—Toscanini and Sibelius. An interviewer once asked her: "Miss Anderson, what was the greatest moment in your life?" Do you know what she answered, this woman of so many great moments? "My greatest moment," she replied, "was the day I went home and told my mother she wouldn't need to take work home anymore." Her greatest moment was associated not with getting but with giving.

We go astray in our quest for happiness because we think of it as something due to us, something the world owes us. Some people we know, are forever complaining, full of grievances against the world because it does not minister to them. The next time you feel this mood sneaking up on you remember you may be suffering from an ingrown ego. Try this prescription. Think of someone at that moment whom you can help. Is there someone whose loneliness you can relieve by a visit? Is there a hospital patient you can cheer with a call? Is there an overdue note of appreciation you can write to someone who helped you over a rough spot? Is there someone hungering for a word of reassurance or encouragement that you can speak? When you are unhappy try doing something for somebody, preferably something involving some inconvenience and time. Life will wear a brighter face when you do because as you give happiness it will come back to bless you.

Meyer Levin, the novelist, made this same observation about the heroine of his latest book, *Eva*. Eva is an 18 year old girl, a Polish Jewess, who miraculously managed to elude the Nazis and to reach ultimate safety in Israel. In a recent issue of the American Zionist, Meyer Levin wrote that the entire gripping episode is unbelievable but true. And he added this comment: "In Eva's story there is an element that is of utmost importance to me. Eva found it hardest to exert herself to survive when she was alone. Only when she was also helping to save someone else, one of the series of close friends with whom she joined forces in each stage of her adventure—only then did her life-urge emerge at its most powerful." In sharing we not only find happiness, we find the will and the power to live.

We cannot dismiss this theme without adding an important

postscript. A vital ingredient of a happy life is the faith that the whole enterprise makes sense, that our lives have a meaning which transcends them and goes beyond our own small life span. Happiness, therefore, involves us not only with each other, but also with God. "Remember us to life, O King, who delightest in life." We are here because God wants us to live and it is He who urges us to fulfill our divinely appointed destiny by living life fully and profoundly. My life is terribly important because it comes from God. I dare not do with it less than my God-given best.

As a Jew I know that living life at its best means being intimately concerned with the destiny of my people, the fate of Israel, the strength of the Jewish community. I die a little bit if I deny their claim upon me and my loyalty to them. Rooted in the soil of my people, I draw strength, sustenance and stature.

Living life at its best means adorning it with the mitzvot of a beautiful tradition. It means Shabbat and prayer, Pesach and Kiddush, Torah study and giving tzdakah. My life becomes hollow and denuded when these fall away. With these as a part of my life, living becomes a holy and meaningful pilgrimage.

Living life at its best means keeping on speaking terms with my conscience, to do nothing to outrage it or to inflict pain upon it. When my acts do violence to my moral or ethical standards, I sustain a loss for which no pleasure nor material gain can compensate me, for I shrink in moral stature. When I keep my friendship with the best in me, I achieve a serenity which cloaks life with gentle beauty.

Happiness then, dear friends, is distilled from the way we live with one another, with our people, with our heritage and with ourselves. And so, when we pray "Remember us to life," we add, "O King who delightest in life." We want the kind of life in which God can take delight. If God finds delight in our lives, we find life delightful. We will find it happy. God grant us all the wisdom to strive for that kind of life on the New Year.

PREPARING FOR OLD AGE

Each passing year finds the human life span prolonged. We have more old age to anticipate than any previous generation. How shall we prepare for it? Economic security is of course basic. But we need other things as well.

Preached on Yom Kippur, 1954
Appeared in The Torch, Fall of 1955

16

Preparing for Old Age

SOME TIME AGO I was visiting at the home of a friend shortly after the death of her aged father. During the course of our conversation she made a wistful remark which bore heavy overtones of regret. "You know," she said, "we ought to give a lot more thought than we do to the problem of preparing for old age."

The bereaved daughter's remorseful remark constitutes a challenge to consider a problem which happily is facing an ever-increasing number of people in our country. One hundred years ago, the life expectancy in our country was age 30. Today it has risen to age 66. Already some 13% of the American population, or more than 20 million people, have passed their sixtieth birthday. By 1980 it is estimated that some 20% of the population will be above that age.

A reflection of this trend is to be found in the emergence of a new science called *geriatrics* which is concerned exclusively with the aging process and its attendant problems. Geriatrics, as I see it, is the answer of science to mankind's perennial prayer. We all want to live long but none of us wants to be old. Geriatrics I think tries to satisfy both seemingly contradictory desires simultaneously.

Now, we must admit at the outset that we cannot speak of "old age" without a number of qualifications. For one thing, when does old age begin? Well, that depends upon whose age we're talking about—our own or our neighbor's. Most of us tend to grow old about 15 years later than the people we know. When

179

one U.S. Senator became a grandfather for the first time, he was asked how he liked his new status. "I love it," he answered like a doting grandfather. "But," he added wrily, "it is somewhat distressing to have to live with a grandmother."

Yes, "old age" is relative. When Earl Warren was appointed Chief Justice in 1953, one of the reasons given for the choice was "his relative youth"—62. On that very day, the governor of Puerto Rico pardoned a prisoner on account of "his advanced age"—63. In baseball, a player is old at thirty-five. For congregational committees in search of a rabbi, old age begins at forty—with the candidates. And Dr. John Erdman, a prominent surgeon, was more in demand at eighty-five than ever before in his life.

Moreover, we do not grow old evenly, the different parts of our body do not age at the same pace. A physician will tell us that a 60 year old man may have a 50 year old kidney, a 40 year old heart, 70 year old liver and he may be trying to live a 30 year old life.

There is also, as we know, a difference between chronological age and emotional age. Some there are who are the perpetual adolescents, petrified youths, who fell in love with an earlier period of life and subconsciously vowed never to part from it. "O moment stay, thou art fair!" they exclaimed with Faust and at that point their growth became arrested.

Notwithstanding these reservations, for our purposes we can define old age as I once heard Walter Reuther define it—that time in life when we are too old to work and too young to die. How should we prepare for old age?

Well, the first thing that comes to people's minds when we speak of preparing for our twilight years, is economic security. We think in terms of pensions, social security, retirement funds, annuities, insurance policies. These are the means we try to adopt to forestall the day when we might find ourselves lacking both physical resources and financial resources. And there is no minimizing the importance of such planning and the peace of mind it affords. It is wise indeed that we do our best to answer the prayer which we repeat regularly in the grace after meals: "Please, O Lord, make us not dependent upon the gifts of human beings." "*Nit onzukummen zu mentchen*" is the way our grandparents prayed in their daily speech.

And yet in old age as in our youth, economic security is never a guarantor of contentment. "Money" it has been correctly observed "is an article which may be used as a universal passport to everywhere except heaven and as a universal provider of everything except happiness." All of us know some aged people who certainly have much more than the modest food and comfort their diminished appetites require and yet they are disgruntled, complaining, miserable.

What else then ought we to bring to old age besides economic security?

One of the most important things each of us should try to bring to old age is an unsoiled and untroubled conscience. At that stage in life when our physical power ebbs and we live more and more with our thoughts, let us make certain that we will not be tormented with the memory of evils perpetrated and hurts inflicted.

This, as we will recall, is the central theme of Sholom Asch's novel, "A Passage in the Night." Isaac Grossman, a one-time immigrant, has made a fortune and controls an empire of hotels and theatres. We find him vacationing in Florida when the book opens. He has everything, it seems, that a man would need in old age. He has more money than he can use, he has prestige, he has the smug self-satisfaction which success often breeds, he has children and grand-children. But he has no peace of mind. For weighing like a mountain on his heart is the searing memory of the Polish worker, Yan Kovalsky, from whom young Isaac Grossman took $27.00 years ago. That was the $27.00 Kovalsky had intended to use for the purchase of a second-hand suit for his daughter's wedding. That was the $27.00 Isaac had needed to begin him on a traveling salesman career which was eventually to lead him to his millions. It is this memory which haunts old Mr. Grossman now and fills him with an obsessive, almost pathological, compunction to try to find the man he had wronged many years ago and to make amends to him. But Yan Kovalsky is not to be found and Isaac Grossman goes from one frustrating quest to the other until his own children begin to suspect his sanity and have him committed to a mental hospital.

Here we may have an extreme example for Isaac's offense was only a single lapse and Judaism does believe in atonement. But what of those who pile ruthlessness upon dishonesty, to whom no relationship is sacred, no loyalty binding, no morals restraining, who are unmoved by sympathy, who rarely yield to a charitable impulse—how serene an old age do they have a right to expect?

Our sages were exceedingly wise. When they wanted to indicate how the young years could be used with greatest profit they said: "Well spent is our youth if it does not bring shame to our old age." For they understood well that the transgressions of youth are loans upon old age payable with interest about thirty years after date. Max Ehrmann's prayer touches upon a most vital need for our advancing years. "May my thoughts and actions be such as shall keep me friendly with myself."

God grant us in old age the blessing of an untroubled conscience.

In the third place, we ought to try to bring to old age an unclosed mind. Someone has said that "Some minds are like concrete; all mixed up and permanently set." The latter part is a danger to which we become more vulnerable as we grow older. It is tempting to develop a permanent mind set.

To shut the windows of the mind is to court mental and spiritual suffocation. Leonardo da Vinci who lived to a ripe old

182

age and continued to paint masterpieces in old age declared, "Learning keeps the soul young and decreases the bitterness of old age." We must literally never stop going to school, broadening our horizons and expanding our knowledge. This after all is the distinctive Jewish contribution to mental hygiene. The unparalleled emphasis of Judaism upon study as a process which only death ought to terminate, spelled out more than a religious duty. It was the key to the fulfillment of the blessing the Torah confers upon its devotees. Thus did the Jew find in it "length of days and years of life"—meaningful days, throbbing years.

The Talmud tells a story about Judah bar Ilai, a second century sage, who deeply impressed a pagan in the market place by his radiant face. "This man" said the pagan, "must either be intoxicated or he has just discovered a hidden treasure." Rabbi Judah overheard him and said: "Stranger, I do not drink except when I must for ritual purposes. When I drink the four prescribed cups of wine on the Seder night, I have a seven-week headache which lasts until *Shavuot*. Neither have I found any treasure. I am a poor man."

"Then what makes your face shine so? How do you manage to look so youthful?"

"That is quite simple." Rabbi Judah answered: "I study all the time. I study the Torah and the quest for knowledge makes the face of a man to shine."

As long as we keep our minds open and alert, as long as we are willing to try a new skill, entertain a new thought, develop a new friend, surrender an old prejudice—so long do we remain vital people, so long do we gain ground and move forward in the search for more abundant life.

God grant us in old age the blessing of the unclosed mind.

Fourthly, we ought to try to bring to old age an undaunted spirit.

The plain fact is that very many of us are literally afraid of growing old. We picture ourselves in old age like "a marooned sailor watching the ship in which he once served disappearing behind the skyline." There are many symptoms of this fear. The fact that cosmetics is today a billion dollar industry is one of them. The billboards and daily newspapers carry advertisements which make old age appear not as a stage of life but as a betrayal of it.

William Lyon Phelps once wrote about the alarm with which we greet the first gray hair. He went on to say: "Now one really ought not to be alarmed when one's hair turns gray; if it turned green or blue, then one ought to see a doctor. But when it turns gray that simply means that there is so much gray matter in the skull that there is no longer room for it; it comes out and discolors the hair. Don't be ashamed of your gray hair, wear it proudly like a flag. You are fortunate in a world of so many vicissitudes, to have lived long enough to earn it."

Now, one does not necessarily have to share Dr. Phelps' passionate love for gray hair. If we happen to prefer another color, today I suppose we have a choice and if another color makes us more cheerful, we are each entitled to our personal preference. But Dr. Phelps is entirely correct in sounding the caution against permitting the advancing years to plant the seeds of fear in our hearts. There has been monotonous repetition and widespread acceptance of the erroneous conception that life reaches its climax in youth. Dr. Phelps recalls that when he was an undergraduate he heard a distinguished gentleman say to the students with emphasis: "Young gentlemen make the most of these four years; for they are the happiest years you will ever know." "That remark" he goes on to say "was given to us with that impressiveness that so often accompanies falsehood. My classmates and I have been out of college nearly 40 years; most of us are happier now than then."

Consider what it would really mean if it were true that "youth is the happiest time of life." If that were truly so, then nothing would be sadder to look at than a young man of 25. For here we would see someone who had reached the very peak of existence, the absolute height and now could only expect decay, decline and descent into the valley. This would be the greatest insult to human personality.

If we are to face the advancing years with serenity and hope we must realize that God has arranged human life on an ascending scale and that every age has its unique satisfactions and joys, just as every hour of the day has its own charm and loveliness. Being a father is wonderful. Being a grandfather isn't bad either. Being a great-grandfather may be even more exciting. True, old age is physical autumn but it can be a spiritual springtime. This is probably what George Santayana had in mind when he said: "Never have I enjoyed youth so thoroughly as I have in my old age."

God grant us in old age the blessing of the undaunted spirit.

For the last, I have left what I consider to be the most precious freightage we must bring to old age—and that is faith in God and in the reasonableness of His work.

Prince Albert, upon his death bed, is reported to have said: "I have had wealth, rank and power. But if this were all I had, how wretched I should be now."

There must be a great emptiness in the heart of a man who comes into the twilight of his life without the assurance that his life is not to be wasted, erased from the black-board of life as though it never existed. How depressing it must be to believe that we have been plodding laboriously along the highway of life only to find that it leads to a dead end.

On the other hand, how soothing is the Jewish faith that "this world is only a vestibule before the palace of eternal life," or, as

Edwin Markham put it: "The few little years we spend on earth are only the first scene in a divine drama that extends on into eternity."

The belief in the indestructability of the human soul has been one of the most passionate and persistent affirmations of all men. Philosophers and physicians, sages and scientists, poets and peasants, are all included in the mighty assemblage who answer "present" when the roll is called among the believers that death is not the end. And the more we have learned about the mysterious universe in which we live, the more persuasive have become the intimations of our immortality.

God has not endowed us with a single craving without providing us with the means of satisfying it. Every natural desire is met by the great commissary of the universe. If we hunger, there is food. If we crave for love, there are human beings to gratify that need. Can it be that our yearning for immortality alone must remain unsatisfied? Does the universe which responds to our every other need, deceive us only here? Is God a cruel prankster? Our craving for immortality in a world which satisfies our every other fundamental need and yearning points to a God who, in the words of our prayer-book, "implanted within us everlasting life."

Yes, we who believe in God cannot look upon His finest and most sensitive creation, the human being, as a "bit player" who speaks a brief stammering line on the earthly stage and then is doomed to eternal silence. Rather do we regard life here as a prologue to a magnificent drama written by the divine Playwright.

> "Come grow old along with me
> The best is yet to be.
> The last of life for which the first was made."

God grant us in old age the blessing of faith in Him and in His wisdom.

PREPARING FOR OLD AGE

Someone has complained that about the time we learn to make the most of life, the most of it is gone. It need not be so. Now is the time to begin to prepare for old age. Old Koheleth, who seems to have known only too well the path that leads to cynicism, placed a helpful marker on our road of life when he advised: "Remember thy Creator in the days of thy youth." Yes, we should give thought to preparing *visible* means of support—but let us not forget to develop *invisible* means of support. Now is the time to keep that conscience clear, that mind open, that spirit courageous, that faith strong.

Henry van Dyke has summed up our theme in a poem which is also a prayer:

> Let me but live my life from year to year,
> With forward face and unreluctant soul.
> Not hurrying to, nor turning from the goal;
> Not mourning for the things that disappear
> In the dim past, nor holding back in fear
> From what the future veils; but with a whole
> And happy heart, that pays its toll
> To youth and age, and travels on with cheer.
>
> So let the way wind up the hill or down,
> O'er rough or smooth, the journey will be joy;
> Still seeking what I sought when but a boy,
> New friendship, high adventure, and a crown,
> I shall grow old, but never lose life's zest,
> Because the road's last turn will be the best.

REKINDLING A SENSE OF DUTY

A dramatic incident in American history mirrors the mood of our time and also points to what must be done in our own ominous days. The advice harmonizes with one of the basic concepts of our faith.

Preached on Kol Nidre, 1961

17

Rekindling a Sense of Duty

L IKE MOST OF my colleagues, I have always found preaching
on the High Holy Days a gravely earnest and almost terrify·
ing responsibility. Months before these "days of awe" are upon
us, they send an agitation into our hearts. Indeed, it would almost
be correct to say that no rabbi really "enjoys" a summer vacation.
No matter what pose of relaxation his body assumes, his mind
is held in a tyrannical grip by the challenging assignment that lies
ahead. My own favorite nightmare finds me standing before the
congregation without a single word to say. In some of my more
whimsical moments I have thought how lovely life would be if
the High Holy Days would come in June and be followed by a
vacation.

One of the obvious reasons why these days cast their heavy
shadows before them is the realization that they offer us the
opportunity to touch so many lives at once, and to touch them
at a time when they are most susceptible to the influence of the
pulpit. Moreover, for too many of these lives, these sermons may
have to do for a long time.

This year, dear friends, I confess that I found the prospect of
speaking on these days more frightening than ever before. As the
international tension kept mounting over Berlin, with each side
becoming progressively more adamant in its position and stronger
in its language, as diplomatic notes became more heavily punc-
tuated with reminders of the devastating power that lay behind
them, the ghastly realization was dawning that we are living in
a very inflammable world and a lot of grown children are playing

with matches. During the last few months there has been a sickening awareness that we and all we love and all we possess can be erased in one blinding moment. What sense does preaching make at a time like this? Sermons deal with enduring values but we ourselves may not endure! A sermon takes a long look at life but how far ahead do we have a right to look? It is not only that the future is uncertain. We are uncertain whether there is to be a future. Bertrand Russell's new book is entitled: *Has Man A Future?* This is a question which gnaws at the hearts of all sensitive people today.

It is in this soul-searching mood that I came upon a dramatic incident in American history which not only provided justification for a sermon but also the theme for it.

The event took place in Hartford, Connecticut during the anxious days of the Revolutionary War. The year was 1780. The day was the 19th of May. On that day, pious New Englanders could not be blamed for believing that the world was coming to an end. For that day dawned bright and clear, but at noon the blue skies turned to ash grey and by mid-afternoon their color was a dense, ominous black. As simple folk who had frequently listened to sermons about the coming of Judgment Day, they were certain that this was it. In their fears they prayed and begged for a final blessing before the world came to its end.

At that very hour, the State Legislature was in session. The Lower House adjourned its meeting in panic. In the State Senate a motion was made for immediate adjournment. Above the din, there was heard the voice of one Colonel Abraham Davenport who arose to oppose the adjournment and then added these measured words: "The Day of Judgment is either approaching or it is not. If it is not, there is no cause for adjournment. If it is, I choose to be found doing my duty. I wish therefore that candles may be brought."

Dear friends, this is indeed a time for bringing candles and of all the candles that we could bring in our day perhaps none is so vital for the survival of all we hold dear than the rekindling of a strong sense of duty. Webster's dictionary defines duty as "the natural, moral or legal obligation to follow a certain line of conduct, or to do a certain thing; the force by which such obligation controls one's will or actions." Duty speaks of obligations and the willingness to permit these obligations to control our actions.

This is not an overly popular doctrine in our time. The towering uncertainty of our times, and the precariousness of our very civilization, appear to have triggered a stampede away from duty, away from responsibility. This seems to be especially true of our young people. Here for example is a round-up of some news reports on how Labor Day week-end was spent by some of America's youth.

Lake George, N.Y.—Capping a three-day drinking spree, about 1,500 college students and other young vacationers, armed with bottles and beer cans, fought police, firemen and civil defense officials. The county jail was filled to overflowing. "I have never seen anything like this," said the Lake George police chief.

Ocean City, Md.—Snarling police dogs helped officers break up an after-midnight gathering of 2,000 youths. Policemen were taunted and pelted with pennies when they ordered the crowd to disperse. Some youths had driven into town in cars bearing signs that read, "Fill your flask and come to the second annual Ocean City riot."

Clermont, Ind.—State troopers, deputy sheriffs and civil-defense police were needed to scatter 150 youths who roamed the streets chanting, "We want booze, we want beer!" The demonstration was against a State law banning the sale of liquor and beer on Sunday.

Hyannis, Mass.—In this Cape Cod town, a few miles from

President Kennedy's summer home, 140 young people were arrested for drunkenness or disorderly conduct.

Wildwood, N. J.—A record number of arrested youngsters— 247, including a number of minors, jammed the jail here. Eight youths were fined $105 each for wrecking a hotel by punching holes in walls, ripping doors from their hinges, smashing windows, hurling ash trays and fire extinguishers.

Before we vent all our righteous indignation upon our young people however, we might pause to ask where were the parents of these young people on this week-end? How seriously were they fulfilling their parental duty if their children were filling the police stations and the jails.

Nor is it only among our young people that the concept of duty is an unpopular and infrequently invoked ideal in our time. To say "yes" to duty often means to say "no" to ourselves; and while we may have heard the ancient Greek counsel urging "know thyself," we rarely hear the advice "no thyself." The dominant slogan in our time has been put to music. "Enjoy Yourself."

Who is brave enough to invoke such old-fashioned concepts as self-discipline, self-control, self-sacrifice, self-denial? The entire emphasis in our time is on self-satisfaction, self-indulgence, self-pampering. All the labor-saving gadgets, all the comfort increasing devices, all the slogans on the bill-boards and commercials— all these conspire to give us the false impression that we are here not to serve but to be served, not to contribute but to consume, not to achieve but to have fun. We tend to think not in terms of obligations but of opportunities. The stern voice of duty has been reduced to an almost inaudible whisper. Is a people raised and nurtured on the pleasure principle big enough and strong enough for the demands of these fateful days? Or must we with all haste and by every means kindle in every heart the neglected candle of duty?

During the past summer we had a melancholy but pointed

illustration how evil men have been able to exploit a sense of duty for their own malevolent purposes. The Nazi hangman on trial for his life in Jerusalem, the first despoiler of our people to undergo trial by Jewry, has built his entire defense on a single premise. He is not responsible for anything because as a loyal citizen of the Third Reich he was simply fulfilling his duty. He was under orders. His not to question why. When the prosecuting attorney Gideon Hausner turned to him and asked him: "What would you have done if you were given an order to kill your own father, would you have carried it out?" he answered: "Yes." He was under orders.

As I read this blood-chilling answer I said to myself, he says he is under orders and I as a Jew am under orders. That is what being a Jew really means. At thirteen a boy becomes a Bar Mitzvah. The primary and dominant meaning of the word *mitzvah* is commandment or order. When he attains his religious majority, the Jew comes under orders. The *mitzvot* are his orders. But what a difference between the orders by which this Nazi demon lived and by which I and you are asked to live! His orders brought on a holocaust. Our *mitzvot* could create a heaven. But do we have the same loyalty to our *mitzvot* as he had to his satanic orders? Do we have the same sense of duty to bring life, and beauty, and holiness as he had to spread death and beastliness and horror?

A phrase which occurs hundreds of times in the High Holy Day liturgy is *Avinu Malkaynu*, "Our Father, Our King." In these two designations of God, we have spelled out our two-fold relationship to Him. Because He is our Father, who loves His creatures, all His creatures, we are each endowed with a noble *yichus*, invested with supreme status, clothed with highest sanctity. But God is not only *Avinu*. He is also *Malkaynu*—our King. A king expects his subjects to carry out and fulfill many fundamental obligations. Thus to speak of God as both our Father and our King is to remind ourselves repeatedly that we are not only

195

endowed with certain unalienable rights but also with certain inescapable duties.

Nowhere is this truth made more vivid than in the *Shema*, perhaps the best known of all our prayers. Now what do we say in the Shema? First, we remind ourselves of our cardinal belief that the Lord our God is One, our uncompromising monotheism. Having made this declaration, we proceed at once to spell out the duties that flow from that affirmation. "Thou shalt love the Lord thy God with all thy heart, with all thy soul, with all thy might. Thou shalt teach these words to thy children. Thou shalt talk of them when thou sittest in thy house, when thou walkest by the way, when thou liest down and when thou risest up. Thou shalt bind them upon thy hand. They shall be for frontlets between thine eyes. Thou shalt write them upon the door-posts of thy house and upon thy gates." Here is an entire prayer concerned exclusively with our duties, the orders under which you and I find ourselves as *B'nai Mitzvah*.

This spirit of our prayers was accurately captured by one mother who overheard her son's prayer in which he listed the many things he wanted the Almighty to deliver to him, preferably before the week-end. She interrupted his prayers by remarking: "Don't give God so many orders. Just report for duty." The primary purpose of prayer is not to issue orders but to accept them.

One of our most crying needs is the need to report for duty. We need it as husbands and as wives. For how secure are the pillars of a home if they are not cemented by a mutual awareness that there are no privileges without corresponding responsibilities? Our growing children need to be given a sense of duty or run the risk of being unprepared for living in the world of reality which will not cater to them free of charge, nor coddle them nor indulge them. As Americans in these days of unprecedented peril we must wake up to the unpopular truth that we not only enjoy a Bill of Rights but also possess a Bill of Duties. If we shirk our duties we shall soon forfeit our rights. It was this thought that President Kennedy had in mind when he said in his inaugural address that Americans should not ask what their country can do for them but rather what they can do for their country.

The words of the 19th century English biologist Thomas Huxley shine with added brightness in our own times. "Perhaps the most valuable result of all education" he wrote, "is the ability to make yourself do the thing you have to do, when it ought to be done, whether you like it or not. It is the first lesson that ought to be learned."

Tonight, dear friends, on this Kol Nidre night when our thoughts turn especially to the household of Israel, I want to suggest that if Judaism is to have any real relevance in our lives, perhaps our most desperate need is to return to the hallowed Jewish concept of *mitzvah*, of duty, of being under orders. We have to recapture the fundamental Jewish concept that there are certain things that we have to do, when they ought to be done, whether we like it or not.

Judaism is not a way of feeling. It is a way of living. It consists of "thou shalts" and "thou shalt nots." They are not always easy to perform. It is not always convenient to perform them. But when there is a conflict between our comfort and our conscience, our convenience and our commandments, our desires and our duties, are we or are we not capable of rising above the behavior of spoiled children? Are we able to say no to ourselves? Are we able to say yes to duty?

These questions touch upon every area of Jewish living but tonight I should like to single out two areas for special consideration.

The first concerns the manner in which our religious occasions are being celebrated. In every Conservative congregation in our

197

city, tonight, the rabbi is reading a statement on this subject drawn up by the Philadelphia Branch of the Rabbinical Assembly. That statement will be published in full in the local Anglo-Jewish press. It will appear in the next issue of the Temple Sinai News. I will confine myself this time to reading a few of the more vital passages.

"Two of the most hallowed Jewish institutions, which we deem indispensable for the survival of Judaism are *Shabbat* and *Kashrut*. To violate either or both of these sacred traditions in conjunction with the celebration of a religious event such as a Bar Mitzvah or a wedding is to compromise seriously the significance of the occasion and to render a disservice to the tradition which provides the motivation and the framework for that occasion.

"Accordingly we call upon all our people to enhance the spiritual character of these sacred moments in their lives by observing them in a manner which honors both the *Shabbat* and *Kashrut*."

In the statement we also announce that the "Kosher Caterers have agreed that on their premises on the Sabbath, they will permit no smoking, candle lighting, photography or music (other than vocal) at functions sponsored by Jewish families or Jewish organizations. At functions which they cater off their premises in public gathering places, they will likewise not permit any of the above infractions on the Sabbath. We (the rabbis) for our part, will not attend or officiate at any time at functions catered by kosher caterers who permit any of the above violations."

At this time, dear friends, I wish to express the hope that the entire Temple Sinai family will honor this appeal and that we will mark the *simchot* God will enable us to celebrate in a manner which will hallow His Name and bring honor to our people and to our heritage.

The second area which I feel merits our special consideration on this, the holiest night on our calendar, is one which I discussed with our sons and daughters at the Friday Night service last April at which we celebrated the Bar Mitzvah anniversary of Israel's independence. At that time I focused attention upon a problem which many of the most competent observers of the Jewish scene consider one of the foremost problems, if not the foremost problem, confronting us in America—the short-circuiting of the Jewish educational process at the unripe age of thirteen. At the age of thirteen, the Jewish student who began studying at the age of eight has actually spent in the religious classroom in the five years only a trifle more than the number of hours he spends in the public school classroom in one year. And remember, on two of the three school days, the religious school gets the child very late in the afternoon with his absorptive capacity reduced, his attention dulled and his body tired. All in all, at the age of thirteen, the pupil has scarcely achieved the kind of religious education a 4,000 year old tradition deserves, and living as a Jew in a Christian society demands.

In addition, it is precisely during the turbulent teen years, when so many profound and painful changes are taking place inside our sons and daughters that they need most the guidance, the fellowship, the values the religious school offers. I therefore appealed to our young people to utilize Israel's Bar Mitzvah anniversary to score a breakthrough in the solution of the Bar Mitzvah problem here in America.

But of course they alone cannot solve the problem. We must all help them. The Rabbi will have to find more time to give them, our School Committee will have to devote special attention to them, our teachers will have to bring deepened devotion to them, and we, their parents, will have to fulfill one of our primary duties by giving them firm guidance and understanding counsel. The major premise in all our discussions must be

199

that the study of Torah is one of our major *mitzvot* and at the time when a boy becomes a Bar Mitzvah and a girl a Bat Mitzvah, they are "under orders." The title spells duties and the first sign of maturity is the recognition of duty and fulfilling it. Our duty as their parents is to help them to see where their duty lies and then give them all the encouragement to be faithful to it.

And so let us pray:

Avinu Malkaynu, Our Father, Our King.

In a world darkened by the black clouds of peril, grant us the courage to kindle the bright candles of duty. Keep us ever mindful that we are B'nai Mitzvah, under orders from Thee, to do what must be done, when it must be done.

Make us big enough to recognize our duties, strong enough to perform them, so that we may know the serenity which comes to those who do Thy will.

May our lives reflect honor upon our people and bring glory to Thy name.

Thus will we do our part towards the building of a better tomorrow for all Thy children everywhere.

REMEMBRANCE ROCK

The Jew cherishes personal memories distilled from his own past and also collective memories drawn from the past of his people. What are some of our most hallowed memories? How are these memories to be translated into our daily lives?

Preached on Yom Kippur, 1962

18

Remembrance Rock

AMONG CARL SANDBURG'S literary works there is a sprawling novel called, *Remembrance Rock*, which breathes the clean fresh air of healthy patriotism. Its central character is Judge Orville Brand Windom, a thoughtful and sensitive man. The title of the book, *Remembrance Rock*, refers to a tall rugged boulder which stands in the center of the Judge's cedar-shaded garden. He likes to go there to meditate from time to time because he has placed some precious dust under the rock. First he put there a handful of dust from Plymouth, Massachusetts in honor of the pilgrim fathers. Alongside it he placed a Colonial silver snuffbox filled with earth from Valley Forge. Then came a little box of soil from Cemetery Ridge at Gettysburg where his father fought, and side by side with that, a handful of earth which he brought back from the Argonne in France where his son fell in the first World War. This precious dust he has reverently gathered around his Remembrance Rock because he does not want to forget the hard road over which this great nation has come.

This Yizkor hour is for us a huge Remembrance Rock in time. It stands at the center of our most tender sentiments. To it, we have each brought in the clenched fist of memory some dust which is personally sacred—the dust beneath which a loved one sleeps, the dust we have moistened with our tears, hallowed by our love. In this sense the Yizkor hour is a most intimate and private moment. A daughter remembers her mother, a wife her husband, a father his son. Remembering, like sorrowing, is a profoundly solitary experience. We recall, as we weep, alone.

And yet there are strong bonds that draw us to each other even in our aloneness. For one thing, we are part of one congregation, listening to one voice, and we will soon join in one prayer. We are sitting together, we will rise together, and together we will each try, with varying degrees of success, to stifle our sobs.

Much stronger than these physical bonds, however, are the firmer though invisible bonds of memories which link us to each other as Jews. In addition to our individual memories as members of a family, we have collective memories as members of our people. The same prayerbook which contains the prayers into which we will soon insert the names of our own beloved dead also contains the prayers which evoke the names of our common ancestors: Abraham, Isaac and Jacob, Moses and Aaron, Rebecca and Hannah, Isaiah and Jeremiah, and the ten martyrs who died al kiddush haShem. Under our Remembrance Rock there is, as under Judge Windom's rock, soil which is sacred to us as individuals and soil which our people's past has sanctified. And today, on this Day of Atonement, when we feel most intensely a sense of "at-one-ment" with each other and with fellow Jews throughout the world. I should like to gather together some precious Jewish bags of soil and consider briefly the lessons that each has to offer.

The first bag of soil that we Jews keep under our Remembrance Rock comes from the slave pits of Egypt. "And you shall remember that you were a slave in the land of Egypt." In no less than fifty passages in the five books of Moses alone, Egypt is the geographical point of reference. In the Ten Commandments, in the grace after meals, in the Kiddush of the Sabbath and festivals, we remember Egypt. On Passover we take our entire families with us on an annual eight-day excursion back to Egypt. We re-enact the drama and try to recapture even the bitter taste of bondage and the salty flavor of the slave's tears. Why this excessive fixation upon the painful chapter in our earliest history?

The answer I feel gives us a clue to the genius of our people. We are a people who learned very early how to utilize every experience creatively, to distill from every event, no matter how barren and forbidding it appeared, some vital lesson. Indeed, we learned that there are certain lessons which are taught only in the school of suffering and that if we mastered these lessons well even our suffering need not have been in vain.

And so in Egypt we digested with our bread of poverty, the understanding of what it means to be denied and downtrodden. Slavery taught us sympathy for those who are stripped of their manhood, compassion for those who toil without hope. The taskmaster's lash which scarred our bent backs burned into our souls the fearful awareness that cruelty not only degrades the slave, it also dehumanizes the master.

These are lessons we are often tempted to forget during these fateful days when the American Negro is struggling to harmonize America's deed with the American dream, its great promise to him with its inadequate performance. Too often we consider ourselves uninvolved in this struggle, or what is worse, we sometimes carelessly throw another log of prejudice on the fire of intolerance. Is it for this that we suffered in Egypt?

I recently had a deeply moving experience as I read the report of a colleague who was one of the Freedom Riders who rode into the South in a mixed group of Negroes and Whites using together the eating facilities, the bathrooms, the water-fountains, the buses which were segregated. "I would drink from the Negro water and the Negroes would drink from the white water. I would drink the colored Coca-Colas and they would drink the white Coca-Colas." This was their first task, to disobey the segregation signs.

Their second task was to address groups of Negroes in different Southern communities, to give them hope and courage. "Don't let anyone step on you" he urged them. "Don't let anyone push you down. Stand up like a man. It's better to stand up for one minute—erect—than to crawl on your hands and knees for your whole life."

"I would tell them," he goes on, " 'I am a Jew' and I would stress this. I wanted them to know Jews are fighting for them. 'I am a Jew and I have come to tell you that we understand how you feel. We too have suffered, but by acting to gain our rights as equal citizens, we have gained those rights. You must do the same. We know what hatred and persecution can do, and you are persecuted.' "

As I read these words, I felt that this was the authentic voice of our people talking out of the profound depths of the Jewish soul. These were the sentiments nurtured on the words of the Haggadah which admonish us at every Seder that every Jew must look upon himself as though he personally experienced the anguish of bondage and the joy of liberation. A Jew can never be neutral when human dignity is under attack. To keep the faith with our ancestors, to be true to ourselves, we must lend our voices and contribute our efforts to the ongoing struggle for the extension of human equality and freedom. Our whole history has uniquely sensitized us to make a distinctive contribution to the vitalization of American democracy. Under our Remembrance Rock, a bag of Egyptian soil is indispensable.

A second bag of soil I would bring from Mount Sinai. It was at Sinai that we were given a code by which to live and a purpose for which to live. It was at Sinai that we became a unique and holy people. It was at Sinai that we first heard the immortal words we were destined to speak to all men. It was at Sinai that great heavenly sparks kindled in the Jewish soul an eternal flame by which all humanity has been warmed. "As long as the world lasts," wrote Matthew Arnold, "all who want to make progress in righteousness will come to Israel for inspiration, as the people who have the sense for righteousness most glowing and strongest."

We listen to these extravagant words of praise from a non-

Jewish scholar and we are understandably uplifted. It is astonishing that so small a people should have made so enormous a
contribution. It is immensely gratifying to be able to say with
Chaim Weizmann: "We may be sons of peddlers but we are the
grandsons of prophets." But what are we ourselves doing with
the legacy of Sinai? To what extent are we trying to familiarize
ourselves with it, to learn what guidance it has for our anxious
times, what direction it can offer to a generation which seems to
have lost its capacity for telling right from wrong, what is its
message to a world hovering on the brink of thermo-nuclear self-
annihilation? To what extent do we permit that legacy to shape
our lives? How much evidence of it do we find in our homes, in
our places of business, in our lying down and our rising up? Do
we teach it diligently to our children? Do we speak of it when we
sit at home or walk by the way? How many distinctively Jewish
acts do we perform in a day, a week, a year? "How strange," Dr.
Heschel has exclaimed, "to be a Jew and to go astray on God's
perilous errands." Unless we keep alive the legacy of Sinai, what
meaning is there to the Jewish past, what likelihood is there for
a Jewish future? And if our past is without meaning and our
future without hope, what sense does it make to be a Jew at all?

But we do want to be Jews. That is why we build and support synagogues. That is why we are here today. That is why we
send our children to religious schools. That is why we look for
colleges for our children with a large Jewish population. That is
why we are so relieved when our son informs us that he has found
a "nice Jewish girl." That is why we search out Jewish neighborhoods, Jewish Swim Clubs, Jewish Country Clubs, Jewish organizations and Jewish causes. All this is evidence of our genuine
yearning to perpetuate our Jewishness. This yearning must be
translated daily into positive acts of loyalty. To live on with
dignity, with direction, with distinction, we must draw regularly
upon those unique moral and ethical values which are embodied

in our legacy, values which teach us what to cherish in the world, how to look upon the world, how to live in the world. Every noble instinct within us cries out that we place under our Remembrance Rock a bag of soil from Mount Sinai.

Another bag I would place under our Remembrance Rock but this one would be filled not with soil but with ashes—ashes from the crematoria of Auschwitz and Bergen-Belsen and Dachau.

I know that no one wants to remember the six million. Germany wants to forget, the world would much prefer not being reminded and we ourselves find the whole subject as painful as it is incomprehensible. To invoke the memories of those who perished in the gas chambers, the ovens and in the heaving graves is to reopen unhealed wounds, to raise questions which cannot be answered without a two-fold assault both upon our sanity and our humanity.

But remember the six million we must. That is the very least we owe them—the immortality which remembrance confers. If we do not remember them, they die a second time. Would we not then be accomplices in the program of obliteration the enemy launched? If we say no Yizkor who will be their refuge against oblivion?

Nor is it for their sake alone that we must remember them. The world needs to be reminded. After the close of the Eichmann trial, the New York Times asked editorially: "What was the object and justification of the trial?" The answer it gave to this question is worth pondering. "It was and it is to do all that can be done to eradicate an evil thing out of our civilization . . . a thing so incredibly wicked that it would not have been believable of modern man if it had not actually occurred. This evil, this wickedness began with intolerance and hate in a few men's hearts. It spread until it almost wrecked the world. Now the obligation is to remember, not in hate, not in the spirit of revenge, but so that this spirit cannot ever flourish again so long as man remains on earth. And to this end, let us begin, each of us, by looking into our own hearts."

These are words that could bear reprinting periodically in newspapers throughout the world which has recently witnessed in many places the reappearance of this malignancy. In South America, in South Africa, in Algeria, in Britain, even here at home, the bigots have begun to emerge from the sewers apparently believing that men have forgotten that the last time intolerance "almost wrecked the world." We must never weary of reminding the world of the six million so that there be no repetition of the catastrophic madness.

In some quarters the lesson seems to have been well learned. At the end of August a highly provocative editorial appeared in the weekly, America, which is published by Jesuit priests. The burden of the message was a "warning" to American Jews that their support of the Supreme Court decision outlawing the New York Regents prayer in public schools might lead to an outbreak of anti-Semitism in this country. The statement precipitated a Niagara of protest not only from accredited spokesmen of the Jewish community but, what is most heartening, from respected voices in the Protestant and Catholic communities as well. Particularly noteworthy was the stinging rebuke administered to America, by Commonweal, which is published by Catholic laymen. "If there is any real danger of anti-Semitism among Catholics," Commonweal wrote, "then it is Catholics who ought to be warned. . . . Indeed, 'warned' is too mild a word. They ought to be told as sharply as possible of the sin of any form of anti-Semitism." Commonweal apparently has not forgotten the six million.

We must remember them for their sake, for the sake of the world and not least, for our own sake. Yes, for our own sake. If it is true as I said earlier that we learned how to use our Egypt, so that the agony of slavery was redeemed by the deepened moral sensitivity we derived from it, then we can use even our Dachau if from it we the living derive a deeper loyalty to our people and to our faith.

There are two things, it seems to me, that we can do. In the the first place we need more Jews. We need larger Jewish families. To all young people still planning their families I say: Every Jewish child that is born constitutes our most dramatic frustration of the enemies of our people. Our answer to death is life. *Lo amut kee echeyeh*, "I shall not die but live." This is a great country with plenty of room for healthy children to grow in and no group has given America more intelligent children, more sober and more law-abiding children than we have. As we raise larger families, America will be the richer, our lives will be the fuller, and our people's future more secure.

In addition to needing more Jews we need better Jews—that means us, you and I. With more than one-third of our people destroyed we must each take upon himself an added measure of responsibility. The prayers they might have offered, we must offer. The books they might have created and read, we must create and read. The *Shabbat* candles they would have kindled, we must kindle. The *tzedakah* they would have given, we must give. Every day, in every way, we must be more devout, more devoted, more dedicated. Our honored dead could not save their own lives but if we and all men remember them, they may be able to save and to deepen ours.

Alongside the bag of ashes, we place our last little sack—this one containing soil from the Land of Israel. This little bag of soil has a long and honorable history. One of the most cherished hopes of the Jew in Eastern Europe was that he could spend his last years in the beloved holy land so that he could at the end be laid to rest in its bosom. Understandably, few were privileged to see the fulfillment of this remote hope. The next best thing was to obtain a sack of holy land soil from an occasional traveler. The

Jew who was fortunate enough to obtain it considered it a veritable treasure. Now he could instruct his children to put this soil on his grave so that he could sleep the everlasting sleep under the sacred soil. If the Jew could not be buried in the land itself he could at least have some of the land placed over him at the end of the journey. Thus the bag of soil was something which one set aside for use at death.

In our day, the sack of Israel's soil is a symbol of life—life emerging out of the ashes, life for a people and its language, life for a culture and a religious civilization, pulsating vitality restored to a people upon contact with the earth which had nourished its earliest and most enduring achievements. Suddenly an old people is young again. The winter of annihilation has been followed by the spring of rebirth. The weary, heavy footsteps on the wanderer's road now give way to young, sturdy feet dancing in the valley of Jezrael. The eyes darkened with fear now are ablaze with hope. The bent backs are straight. Israel itself is the most glowing tribute to the six million, for it was born out of their agony, it has welcomed and comforted their surviving kin and above all, it is the most effective defense against a repetition of the holocaust.

And who can find the words to capture what Israel has meant to us? Many of us have already been privileged to behold the miracle of Israel reborn with our own eyes. Thousands of our American young people have walked its dusty roads with a renewed sense of pride. All of us have found new hope, new streams of strength flowing to us in refreshing abundance out of Zion. The bag of its earth becomes for us a witness of the bonds of enduring love which bind us to the Yishuv, to its destiny, to its tomorrow.

This, then, dear friends, is what I would place under our Remembrance Rock. Some soil from Egypt to teach us compassion, some soil from Sinai to reaffirm our convictions, some ashes from the crematoria to strengthen our commitments and some soil from the Land of Israel to proclaim our comradeship with our Israeli brethren. If it is at such a rock that we gather regularly to meditate quietly, then I believe that when the time comes for our loved ones to add the remembrance of us to the memories they cherish, we may be for them a source of tender benediction.

SPACES TO CONQUER

At a time when massive energies and resources are being directed towards the conquest of outer space, it is of crucial significance that we do not overlook other space problems which confront each of us in our personal lives. Yom Kippur is concerned with these human space problems. We should be too. Very much is at stake.

Preached on Yom Kippur, 1963

19

Spaces to Conquer

L AST FRIDAY President Kennedy addressed the United Na
tions. One of the important passages in his speech was an
invitation to the Soviet Union to work with us in sending a man
to the moon, to pool our common knowledge and resources to
conquer space.

The conquest of space is high on humanity's agenda of problems and will be receiving huge sums of money, the finest brains
and vast attention in the immediate future and in the years ahead.
Our children will surely grow up in a world which will witness
enormous further strides towards the conquest of space, if not its
ultimate conquest.

This is a new problem. It did not exist when we were children.
But there is one space problem which is very old—at least as old
as the Prophet Isaiah. In the fifty-ninth chapter we read this indictment: "Your sins have separated between you and your God."
The prophet looks upon sin as something which creates a separa-
tion and estrangement, something which cleaves and alienates. In
brief, sin creates space between man and God.

In a very real sense, Yom Kippur is the day which summons
us to conquer this space created by our sins, to bridge the chasm,
to heal the rift, to unite that which has been separated. Tonight
I want to touch upon some of our vital human space problems.

The first space problem to which this night calls our attention
is the space which we have permitted to develop between ourselves
and our fellowman.

An ancient and hallowed practice among our people during the ten days of penitence was to use the mellowing inspiration and inwardness of these days to ask forgiveness of neighbors, of friends and of relatives. When Kol Nidre arrived and some friends had not yet been spoken to, the last moments before the service began were utilized for that purpose. There was a buzzing in the synagogue and intense movement as the worshippers approached one another and begged forgiveness for any offenses or slights or hurts inflicted knowingly or unwittingly in the past year. This is a practice we would do well to revive. It is a gentle way of conquering the space that develops between us in the course of the jostlings and the frictions and the collisions in the course of a year.

So many families are in need of this practice. Families today are so much smaller than they used to be. We have fewer children than our grandparents had, and we shrink these small families further by nursing our grudges, by harboring smouldering resentments, by magnifying slights, by being incapable of asking or granting forgiveness. Thus we permit space to grow between ourselves and those we should hold close. We violate the wise counsel found in the Jerusalem Talmud: "He who takes vengeance or bears a grudge acts like one who having cut one hand while handling a knife, avenges himself by stabbing the other hand."

One of the most difficult things in the world is to ask forgiveness. It is not easy to admit guilt even to oneself. It is excruciatingly painful to confess guilt to the one against whom we have offended. But if we want to avoid the bitterness which flows from hatred and the poisons which it releases into our systems we must learn how to ask forgiveness so that we might conquer the space that separates us from those whose lives we ought to deepen and who should be enriching our own. Yom Kippur asks us to conquer the space we have permitted to develop between ourselves and our friends, between ourselves and our loved ones. Never

216

mind who started it. Are we big enough to end it? Great are the rewards if we do.

There is another space problem about which Yom Kippur has much to say. I refer to the space which yawns between our principles and our practices, between our consciences and our conduct, between our creeds and our deeds. There are the massive contradictions and the discrepancies, the inconsistencies and the hypocrisies which stain our lives. We talk one way and live another. We embrace lofty ideals and then betray them by our mean acts. Ralph Waldo Emerson spoke directly to each of us when he said, "Go put your creed into your deed." This is advice we don't follow consistently enough or faithfully enough. Too wide is the space between our creeds and our deeds.

We profess a belief in human equality but we harbor prejudice.

We laud democracy because it is a government of law but we seek to avoid the law when it is personally inconvenient.

We extol character but swiftly trade it for a material advantage.

We praise the family but we undermine it by faithlessness.

We are "proud" to be Jews but we give no semblance of Jewishness in our daily lives, in our homes and in our offices.

In the confessional, one of the sins for which we ask forgiveness is, "The sin which we have sinned before Thee in public and in private." Perhaps the sin referred to is the sin that we are talking about—that we are not in private what we pretend to be in public, that we live split-level lives. The integrity which is so indispensable to vital and creative living is thus denied us. We are fragmented and broken when we should be unified and whole.

Let us be frank about this matter. To a certain extent it is inevitable that our ideals out-race our actions. It is in the nature

217

of an ideal that it is something towards which we aspire. Once it is attained it ceases to be an ideal and so it is inevitable that there be some distance between our actual performance and the principles which we profess. This space problem cannot be totally conquered. What is of crucial significance, however, is that we be aware of the space and that we make every effort to bridge it, that we eliminate as far as within our power lies, the gaping abyss that so often grows larger as we grow older. Far from struggling to heal the divide, we so often surrender, we come to terms with inconsistency. We wink at hypocrisy, we cease to be disturbed over the discrepancies which should agitate us profoundly. Yom Kippur has for its prime purpose the shattering of our complacency. It tries desperately to enlist us once again in the struggle so that we might indeed turn our attention to reduce the space which separates our performance from our profession, our action from our diction.

There is another space problem for us to conquer—the space between what we are and what we know we can be.

Among his literary remains Nathaniel Hawthorne left some "Note Books," which contain random ideas he jotted down as they occurred to him. One of the short entries reads as follows: "Suggestion for a story—story in which the principal character never appears." Unfortunately, this is the story of so many lives. The principal character simply never appears. The character we might become, the person we might grow into, the dimensions we might achieve—somehow do not appear. Our potential greatness lies unrealized, the splendor remains imprisoned, the promise unfulfilled. Our lives develop a static character. We are arrested, fixed. We stop growing morally and spiritually and intellectually and esthetically. We do not expand our sympathies. We do not enlarge our interests. We do not further our knowledge. We do not deepen our understanding. We do not strengthen our self-control. We remain essentially where we were last year, five years ago, twenty years ago. Perhaps we have even retrogressed. The space is getting wider and bigger and more frightening.

The redeeming message of Yom Kippur is that this space can be conquered—if not entirely, largely and significantly. The principal character can yet appear if we will it passionately, with all our hearts and with all our souls.

One of the saddest verdicts of spiritual surrender that has come to my attention was a sentence written by the young French novelist, Francois Sagan. "At nineteen," she wrote, "I could have been changed but now I can no longer change the set of reflexes which is me." How old was she when she rendered this despairing judgment? Twenty-four! Well, Judaism does not believe that we cannot change and grow. Yom Kippur does not believe it nor does modern psychology. A noted psychiatrist recently declared, "The whole life of the individual is nothing but the process of giving birth to himself—indeed we should be fully born when we die—although it is the tragic fate of most individuals to die before they are born."

Lewis Mumford has defined man as "the unfinished animal." He affirms that man is "the only animal who is not content to remain in the original state of nature."

In our finest moments we know that this is true. We know that morally we simply have so much more power than we care to use, so much more potential that lies untapped. The fundamental significance of this day is to sound a call to us to use that power, to further the development of the unfinished animal, to make way for the appearance of the principal character who is waiting for us to create him.

For the last, I have left the space problem with which we launched our theme—the space about which Isaiah complained, the space between ourselves and God. It has become commonplace to observe that according to the opinion polls the over-whelming majority of Americans believe in God. The actual sta-tistic was something like 95% who answered "yes" to the ques-tion, "Do you believe in God?" God never had it so good. Never has belief in God been so wide-spread and at the same time, so totally irrelevant to the behavior of the believers, so completely disconnected from life. Apparently, belief in God is a matter of private belief, so private that it does not impinge upon the action of the believer. It spells out no consequences, it demands no commitments. It remains what Coleridge once called "a bedridden truth asleep in the dormitory of the mind."

Last Wednesday evening the newspapers carried a story about a woman who heads an organization called "Other Americans, Inc." She was appealing for funds to construct an information and education center which would disseminate the teachings of her organization. Her organization is avowedly and frankly dedi-cated to propagating atheism. Now America is a free country and every American has the right to be an atheist, thank God. What was of special interest to me was her way of stating the objectives of her organization. "To teach the concept of man living with man rather than living with God." What bothered me was that in our day and age it is possible to draw a distinction between man living with God and man living with man. Can one live with God and be indifferent to how he lives with His creatures? Apparently the image which religion has projected upon the popular mind is that it is possible to draw such a distinction, that living with God does not spill over into the whole domain of living with man. This is a very sad and telling indictment against us.

I wondered, too, where the good lady will be looking for her texts for her lessons. Will she not of necessity turn to the writings of the prophets whose passion for social justice and compassion and brotherhood has never been excelled and who were at the same time the most God-intoxicated men who ever lived? The unique contribution of the prophets was the powerful affirmation that there is to be no space between religion and righteousness; that whether we believe in God is spelled out in our dealings with our fellow men. "The Holy God is sanctified through righteousness."

I would also strike a note of caution for our good lady friend. Let her not be too hasty in excluding God from her deliberations. Our experience with societies who dropped God out of their beliefs and affirmations would seem to indicate that very soon thereafter man didn't do too well either. Exhibit A—Nazism. Exhibit B—Communism.

But it is not to her essentially that I am speaking today. It is to ourselves. It is we who must ask whether we can eliminate God from our lives and not pay heavily for this omission. The widespread breakdown in morality which is eating away at the very structure of our society, the enormous incidence of crime which grows at a frightening annual rate, the ever-increasing number of broken homes and besmirched public reputations, all seem to indicate that there is a very heavy price indeed being paid for the space which is developing between ourselves and our God.

In addition to these very apparent outward developments there are a host of inner, more subtle consequences of this growing estrangement. Professor Louis Finkelstein has written sensitively about this aspect of the problem.

"The restlessness which characterizes us, the confusion which has come on our times, the increasing percentage of neuroses among us, and the general unhappiness of all of us in the midst of the greatest affluence the world has yet seen, has come upon us primarily because of the lack of that sense of communion with God which made our forefathers happy in spite of their poverty and their physical sufferings. We resemble most closely those little

221

children who, not having yet learned to interpret the symptoms of weariness and hunger, cry when bedtime or mealtime comes, and yet refuse either to go to bed or take their food. Living in a gilded palace, as it were, we are still miserable, for we are essentially orphans, having lost that most precious of all values in life, the sense of the Fatherhood of God.

"The feeling of deprivation grows sharper and more poignant, instead of less severe, as we grow older. The time comes to each of us when the burdens fade, and we notice the lengthening shadows which presage our end.

"More than ever then do we become homesick; homesick, not for our houses or for our countries, but homesick for the universal Parent of all of us, for that deep affection which is the heart of the universe itself, for the mercy of God; yet a wall of iron has been placed between us and Him, and we cannot find Him. What greater good can a man achieve either for himself or for the world, than to contribute his effort to piercing this wall, and bring the Father and the children once more into loving communion with one another!"

Yom Kippur urges us most insistently to conquer this space between us and our Heavenly Father.

The greatest affirmation of the Jew is the Shema. God is one! As He is one, we are to strive for oneness, for wholeness, for integrity.

The English name for Yom Kippur is "the Day of Atonement." It has often been observed that the word "atone" can be broken into the words "at one." On this day we are urged above all to become at one with each other, at one with our creeds, at one with ourselves and at one with our Creator. To the extent that we succeed in conquering these space problems, to that extent will this day have fulfilled its purpose in our lives so that every day might find us drawing closer and nearer to all the things for which this day stands.

TEMPTED TO HIGHER THINGS

There are certain temptations which ought not to be resisted. And yet we do. Why? Some of our more popular strategies of resistance are analyzed and then we are summoned to higher things.

Preached on Kol Nidre, 1962

20

Tempted to Higher Things

PHILLIPS BROOKS, one of America's great orators of the 19th century, once said that if he could choose a young man's companions he would choose three kinds. Some who were weaker than he so that he might learn to develop patience and charity; many as nearly as possible who were his equals so that he might enjoy with them the full freedom of friendship; but most should be stronger and better than he so that he might be tempted to higher things.

For our purposes on this Kol Nidre night I want to focus on the last phrase—tempted to higher things. It involves a rather unusual use of the word "temptation." The dictionary defines temptation as "the state of being enticed to evil." In common usage it always has that negative meaning, being drawn down to some unworthy level of conduct. Temptation in moralistic literature is considered an instrument of the devil and it is invariably linked with sin. It is something to be staunchly resisted, something to fight against with all our moral power. But Brooks speaks of being "tempted to higher things." Not only does evil have its magnetic power but goodness also draws us to itself. Just as there are temptations which would debase us, there are temptations which would elevate us. There are temptations to be resisted and temptations to which we should succumb. And at this moment of self-confrontation on this atonement day, we ought to be stabbed by remorse not only as we recall the temptations to lower things for which we were too weak but also the temptations to higher things for which we were too strong.

In a recent issue of the *Saturday Review*, there appeared a poem with the ironic title, "You Too Can Conquer Your Better Nature." The poet (Morris Bishop) recalls not too proudly some "victories" he has scored over the temptation to higher things.

> "My father once bestowed on me a dollar,
> Rewarding some good deed I had not done.
> Should I accept? I struggled with my scruples.
> And I won.
>
> My courage once was publicly commended—
> I had stood fast, too paralyzed to run.
> Should I tell all? I fought my better nature;
> And I won.
>
> When conscience bade me make a full confession,
> Repenting every tawdry fault and sin
> I fought a war with conscience and won it.
> I always win."

This same theme is treated in much more sombre terms by Marguerite Wilkinson in a poem entitled "Guilty."

> "I never cut my neighbor's throat;
> My neighbor's gold I never stole;
> I never spoiled his house and land,
> But God have mercy on my soul!
>
> For I am haunted night and day
> By all the deeds I have not done;
> O unattempted loveliness!
> O costly valor never won!"

She was tempted to higher things but resisted the temptation. Opportunities to be kind confronted her but she let them pass unused. Courage called to her and she pretended not to hear.

Who among us on this night is free from the kind of memories which haunt the poet? A worthy cause appealed for our help. We were tempted to respond to human need out of our abundance, but instead of a gift we offered an excuse. We were present at a gathering where gossip was doing its malevolent work and we were tempted to speak the word to halt the character assassination. But why should we run the risk of being unpopular? We heard a minority maligned by uncomplimentary references to their race or faith. We were tempted to cry out "that's not fair!" Instead we kept a polite silence and permitted the cutting wheels of conversation to grind on. We precipitated a family quarrel, voices were raised, angry words were exchanged, alienation resulted. After the heat has subsided we know that one soft word can restore peace. Inside we ache all over to speak that word. We are sorely tempted to drag those heavy syllables past our lips to heal the hurt in a world which is already too full of hurt, and to wipe away the bitterness in a world bitter enough. But we resist the temptation. The word remains unspoken. The bitterness lingers—a hollow tribute to our victory over our better nature.

A modern minister has cited a particularly poignant incident which dramatizes our extreme capacity to resist to our own hurt the temptation to higher things. Parents of an only daughter opposed her marriage to a young man who was unacceptable in the social circles in which this family moved. He came from "the wrong side of the tracks." The minister himself knew him to be an upright person, full of promise and devotedly in love with the young lady. He tried his best to persuade the parents to attend the wedding. "No," said the mother, "I will not lend myself to it! I will have nothing to do with it!" The minister pleaded warmly and passionately but in vain. The wedding took place in pathetic loneliness. After the ceremony he decided it would be an act of kindness to write to the mother describing the brighter

227

side of the wedding. The next day the mother came to see him, sobbing pitifully: "I don't know why I did it. I wanted to come. Inside of me, I wanted to come. I knew it was right. I nearly did come. But, Oh, God! Oh God! I didn't."

Wanted to come! Nearly did come! Powerfully tempted to higher things, stubbornly resisting the temptation.

The mother is each of us in some measure. Knowing what is good and turning our backs upon it. Being drawn to kindness yet persisting in cruelty. Seeing the food for our hungry spirits laid before us and yet powerless to reach out to take it. Hearing the call to loyalty from a gentle and wise tradition and stuffing our ears with the cotton of lame self-justification. Thus we resist what we should embrace and the loveliness we should have practiced remains unattempted.

Why? Why do we resist the temptation to higher things? Well there are many reasons—and each of us has his own. Often we rationalize, proving to ourselves that our faults are really not faults but shining virtues. This we might call the sin of pretending, picturing ourselves as being quite different than we really are. I read recently a quip about a very expensive surgeon who is also quite compassionate. If a patient cannot afford his operation fee, he offers to touch up the x-rays a bit. We do that you know. Rather than go through the pains of removing an ugly growth upon our character we cover it with some mental cosmetics until it looks downright pretty. We refuse to become involved in community service not because we are too self-centered. No, we are independent thinkers. We cling to old grudges and time-worn resentments not because we are petty. No, we are men of principle. We meddle in other people's affairs uninvited not because we are seized by unhealthy curiosity. No, we are just plain friendly folk. We try to regulate the lives of our children and our mates not because we are domineering. No, we are just doing it for their own good. How can we succumb to the temptation to higher things when we have firmly convinced ourselves that we are already practicing them?

When we are not pretending, we are often projecting, attributing the blame for our actions or inactions upon someone else. This is an old trick. It is as old as Adam. When God reproaches Adam for eating the fruit of the forbidden tree, Adam, like many a husband since, promptly points the accusing finger at his wife. "The woman whom Thou gavest me she did give me of the fruit and I did eat." When God turns to Eve, she points to the snake. "The serpent beguiled me and I did eat." The Bible doesn't carry the interrogation any further but I have often speculated whom the snake would have blamed. Channing Pollock has suggested that the reason why Robinson Crusoe was so delighted when he found his Man Friday was that before then when anything went wrong, he had no one to reproach but himself.

A few years ago when it became known that one of Hollywood's most gifted actresses was carrying a child that was not her husband's, she explained her behavior very neatly: "I couldn't help myself." Just why she couldn't help herself she didn't elaborate. Adolf Eichmann on trial for the brutal liquidation of six million children, parents and grandparents answered in effect: "I couldn't help myself, I was under orders." Under orders to play the beast. An 18 year old held for five robberies and a charge of rape explained himself to the judge by saying: "I'm just built that way. It's in my blood." And so it goes. Blame the genes, blame the dictator, blame the emotions, blame the environment, blame the "circumstances beyond our control," blame anything and anybody but, as a popular song of some years ago pleaded, "don't blame me." Shakespeare's Edmund in *King Lear*, is talking about too many of us when he says: ". . . we make guilty of our disasters the sun, the moon, and the stars: as if we were villains by necessity; fools by heavenly compulsion; knaves, thieves and treachers by spherical predominance; drunkards, liars and adulterers by an enforced obedience of planetary influence." Yes, we say, I am tempted to higher things. How often have I hoped I could get out of the shadows and into the sunlight, liberate myself from the tyranny of the emotions, live at peace with God by day and sleep on the soft pillow of a good conscience by night—but I can't help myself.

There is still another reason why we resist the temptation to higher things. In addition to pretending and projecting we do too much postponing. We are indeed powerfully attracted by goodness. We too hear God's insistent still small voice calling to us. But we're not quite ready to answer; no, not quite yet. One religious teacher confessed in his old age that when he was an undisciplined young man he used to pray to God to make him better. He would, however, speak the prayer softly for fear that God might hear him and answer his prayer too soon. Like too many of us he acknowledged the claim of his conscience but wanted to discharge his obligations with a dated check. We'll be good, O God, but please don't press us too hard. We need more time. We'll become honest in our business but not right now. First we have to take care of all our needs—real and imaginary. We'll start coming to the Synagogue for weekly renewal and some interior redecorating, but not right now. When we retire—yes, then we'll have plenty of time. We'll free ourselves from that enslaving habit—one of these days. O the things we are going to do tomorrow—the breaches in the family wall we will mend, the classes we will join, the services we will render, the passions we will conquer! But in the meanwhile. . . .

The devils, it is reported, were assembled in international convention. The chief order of business was understandably enough how to increase their efficiency in their devilish work. The first speaker declared that he personally found it very useful to persuade people there is no God. "When I convince a man there is no God, I can get him to do almost anything I want." A second speaker had a different approach. "It's too hard to get people to disbelieve in God. Everybody is drawn to a belief in God. I tell them: 'Yes, there is a God but don't believe what the Bible says. You don't have to follow its teachings because it really makes no difference to God.'" The third and wisest of all speakers disagreed with both his colleagues. "I don't try to argue against God or the Bible. I get a man to do what I want by assuring him that there is a God, the Bible is to be obeyed. I grant all that. But then I say to him: 'What's your hurry? You've got time!'"

Yes, we've got time. And so life continues on the same shabby level. We are only a fraction of the persons we could become and we who are morally eight-cylinder people go chugging along on two. Vast resources of soul and spirit remain unused because we postpone acting on the temptation to higher things.

By whatever means we resist the temptation to higher things —and we could enumerate other strategies of resistance—what troubles us is that we never quite succeed in killing that temptation. It is stubborn and persistent. It will not go away and leave us alone. It continues to torment us like it tormented the prophet Jeremiah. He heard a call from God urging him to catalogue to the callous people their countless sins and to warn them of the impending disasters of destruction and exile. Understandably, Jeremiah resisted the divine mandate. He knew very well the exorbitant price of prophecy, the scorn, the resentment, even the physical punishment that are too often the coin with which a community repays those who would remind it of its transgressions. Jeremiah no less than any of us, liked to be liked. He didn't want to be a laughing-stock for fools and a target for men of violence. And so he resisted the temptation to speak out, to deliver the message the people needed so desperately to hear. Was he then at peace? Did the temptation go away? Let Jeremiah tell us what happened.

"And if I say: 'I will not make mention of Him, nor speak any more in His name,' then there is in my heart as it were a burning fire shut up in my bones, and I weary myself to hold it in, but cannot."

The temptation simply would not let him go. You see, we Jews are a stubborn people and we have a stubborn God. He just would not take "no" as Jeremiah's final answer. And so He continued to call to the reluctant prophet, to disturb him by day and to torment him by night until the prophet cried out: "O Lord, Thou hast enticed me and I was enticed, Thou hast overcome me and hast prevailed."

The struggle of Jeremiah has a painfully familiar ring. We each know what he is describing because we too are seized by the unrelenting temptation to higher things. On this night we feel it stronger than ever. On this night our strategies of resistance are more easily exposed for what they truly are—clumsy devices of our little selves who are afraid of growing up.

Those of us who are living behind the masks of pretense find the make-believe so much more difficult to sustain on Kol Nidre night. The bright light of truth shines too fiercely almost compelling us to see ourselves and to confront ourselves as we really are. Its heat melts off the make-up we have applied to cover our soul blemishes. This night pleads with us to take the energy we are now using to disguise what we really are and use it to become what we ought to be.

To those of us who are blaming "circumstances beyond our control" Kol Nidre is a forceful reminder that we human beings are not only creatures of circumstance, we are also creators and masters of circumstance. A perceptive Hebrew adage captures the sublime truth about us. Ayn davar omed bifnay haratzon. "The spirit of man conquers all." We can reach any moral heights we

choose but we must will it with all our hearts, with all our souls
and with all our might.

To those of us who are postponing to some uncertain tomorrow the things that can be done and should be done today,
this Day of Atonement is a call to make haste. Many there were
for whom last Yom Kippur was their last. Do we know how soon
it will be too late? Are we justified in resisting the temptation to
higher things now, when now is all we have with certainty, and
whatever future is coming to us must be richer if we use the
present more wisely?

One thing above all this day does for us. With incomparable
persuasiveness it tempts us to higher things. It reminds us that
we are children of God and our exalted pedigree points to our
potential destination. "Thou hast made man but little less than
divine." In his famous Nobel Prize speech, the late William
Faulkner echoed the conviction of our tradition when he said:
"I believe that man will not merely endure; he will prevail. He
is immortal not because he alone among creatures has an inexhaustible voice but because he has a soul, a spirit capable of compassion and sacrifice and endurance." In brief, man is capable of
higher things.

And more. The God who put higher things within our reach
is also with us as we struggle to attain them. "He who strives for
purification" our sages taught "receives heavenly assistance." God
helps those who genuinely want to help themselves to be what
He has told us we can become.

On this night, dear friends, it is our custom at Temple Sinai
for me to play the role of the tempter to higher things as I urge
that each of us share some measure of his bounty with the Synagogue. Some of us have very little resistance to this temptation.
They love their Synagogue. They feel a strong sense of community obligation. They are aware of their many blessings and

they translate their gratitude to God into a generous gift. Moreover, repeated responses over the years have long since worn down their resistance.

There are others who when they are tempted to give could say as one parishioner said to his rabbi after listening to a personal appeal: "Rabbi, don't forget I have my generous impulses under perfect control." Well, I hope that all of us tonight will let our generous impulses run riot. I am not asking you to give until it hurts. Give until it doesn't hurt—until you realize that through your gift you are not only helping the Synagogue grow but you yourself are growing. For as we succumb to the temptation to higher things we fulfill the destiny God has in mind for us and we become worthy of being His children.

O God who forgives

On this night of atonement,
We are haunted by memories of duties unperformed, promptings disobeyed, beckonings ignored. Opportunities to be kind knocked on the doors of our hearts and went weeping away. We are ashamed, O Lord, of our easy submission to the temptation to lower things, of our stern resistance to the temptation to higher things.

Make us big enough to admit our transgressions; strong enough to forsake them.

Humble us by showing us what we are.
Exalt us with a vision of what we may grow to be.

Kindle within us the warming fires of faith and set aglow our courage to live as we pray.

WHAT IS IN THE MIDDLE OF YOUR LIFE?

So often it appears that the only thing in life which is certain is its uncertainty. But this is far from the whole truth. At the heart of our tradition is a great affirmation. And what a difference it makes!

Preached on Rosh Hashanah, 1955
Appeared in The Torch, Fall of 1957

21

What Is in the Middle of Your Life?

WE HAVE COME to our synagogue on this day of Rosh Hashanah from a world packed with pressure and tight with tension. Today the synagogue appears to us like an island of serenity in an angry ocean. How fittingly might we apply to it the beautiful lines of the poet:

> "In the heart of the cyclone tearing the sky
> And flinging the clouds and the towers by
> Is a place of central calm.
> So here in the rush of earthly things
> There is a place where the spirit sings
> In the hollow of God's palm."

Having torn ourselves away from "the rush of earthly things," and having assembled in this "place where the spirit sings," let us use this moment of spiritual refuge to think together about the major motif of these prayers we have been uttering as well as of the unspoken thoughts which have filled our yearning hearts these past few hours.

We have been praying for nothing less than life itself. However differently we may each look upon it, however diverse the purposes to which we intend to put it, it is life itself, more life, for which we are asking. And our earnestness is commensurate with the prize.

But even while we pray for life, we are all mindful of the perils and uncertainties of life. The very spelling of the word calls attention to the vast contingencies with which life is fraught. In the very middle of the word LIFE, there is IF. In the middle of every life there is a big IF.

Robert Frost makes this point sharply in a haunting little poem called "The Road Not Taken." Once while walking through the forest he came upon a fork where two paths branched out. Naturally, he could take only one but in the poem he wonders what would have happened had he taken the other path.

> "I shall be telling this with a sigh
> Somewhere ages and ages hence
> Two roads diverged in a wood, and I
>   took the one less travelled by
> And that has made all the difference."

A man chooses a road that leads to a career or to the selection of a life's mate or to a crucial decision in his business and then in an introspective moment he thinks of "the road not taken." What would have happened if I had taken the other road. How vastly different my life might be today!

The famous artist Whistler had his heart set upon a career in the army but he was dropped from West Point because he failed in chemistry. In later life he used to say: "If silicon had been a gas, I should have been a major-general."

Yes! The big IF in the middle of every life. How often do you and I in our reveries walk along the road not taken.

Nor is it only our own decisions and our own choices which affect our destinies. During the Nazi holocaust, when European Jewry was being decimated, I would ask myself repeatedly: "What if my father had not made the boat?" My very life hinged literally upon a decision made by my father who could not possibly have been aware at the time of the fateful consequences of his choice.

This thought came back to me a little while ago when I watched on television the dramatic reconstruction of "A Night To

Remember"—the last stirring hours in the life of the proud Titanic. The tragedy claimed the lives of over 1500 people including 102 women and 54 children. After the gripping presentation was over, the narrator added a tone of poignancy to the disaster by saying:

> If the Titanic had heeded any of the 6 iceberg warnings that it had received;
>
> If it had hit the iceberg 16 seconds sooner or 16 seconds later;
>
> If the Californian had heeded the Titanic's agonized cries for help;
>
> If the Titanic had carried more lifeboats;
>
> If its water-tight cabins were one story higher;
>
> If the night were moonlit;
>
> If any of these contingencies had occurred, the disaster might have been averted.

The enormous IFs in the middle of 1500 lives!

Once we realize how central a position IF occupies in our life as we look backwards, it takes only the most superficial reflection to grasp the role of IF in our life as we look ahead. Indeed, overwhelming uncertainty has become the dominant mood of our time. Only at political conventions is the road to the future pictured with dogmatic assurance as peaceful and unbroken. Sober students of our time have with compelling evidence labeled our age as the Age of Anxiety. Living as we do during the era of the alphabetical bombs, we can understand why Quincy Howe has written that "the 20th century has put the human race on trial for its life."

But even apart from the added hazards of this nuclear Age of Anxiety, life at Rosh Hashanah time has always presented a series of big IFs to any Jew who surveyed the year ahead against the background of his prayerbook. On each of the three Holy Days, life's precariousness and perils are spelled out with terrifying realism.

"Who shall live and who shall die
Who shall perish by fire and who by water
Who shall have rest and who shall go wandering
Who shall be tranquil and who shall be disturbed
Who shall be at ease and who shall be afflicted
Who shall become poor and who shall wax rich
Who shall be brought low and who shall be exalted."

The only thing in life, it would appear, of which we may be reasonably certain, is its uncertainty. As we peer into the future, the IF in the middle of life looms large indeed.

And yet, is that all we can say about life? Can it be that the only thing we can say with assurance is that there is nothing we can say with assurance? Is life to be reduced to a series of haphazard contingencies which we are powerless to control and helpless to change? Must life pivot on so unstable a center? Must we face tomorrow with only a huge, baffling question mark to sustain us?

In our innermost hearts you and I know that at the center of our life there can be something more than IF. And that plus, that added element, is indicated by the Hebrew word for life. That word as we know is "chayim." Like its English counterpart, it is also a four lettered word. But what is in the middle of "chayim?" The two middle letters of chayim are two yuds, and two yuds, as we know, spell the name of God.

The antidote to a life befogged by uncertainty is a life rooted in God.

If life is not to sag under the burden of heavy hazards, it must be supported by the stout beams of great affirmations.

IF reduces life to a question mark.
God punctuates life with an exclamation point.

IF makes us helpless bystanders.
God makes us intelligent co-workers.
IF leads to despair,
God whispers courage.

And so, no sooner have we finished reciting all the uncertainties in the *Uvrosh Hashanah* prayer than we exclaim: "But Thou art ever our living God and King." Given God as the vital center of our lives, we can meet every contingency of life without being defeated or overwhelmed. This is the central meaning of these Holy Days. This is the theme of the 27th psalm which is read during this entire penitential season. "The Lord is my light and my salvation, whom shall I fear? The Lord is the stronghold of my life, of whom shall I be afraid?"

Let us see what it means to put God at the center in times of trouble. Does it mean that faith in God grants us and our children immunity to polio, keeps us from crippling accidents or assures us uninterrupted prosperity? To be sure, there are some people whose faith is as naive as that. They are what we might call God's fair-weather friends. When the sun of good-fortune smiles down on them, they are enrolled among the believers. But let a heavy cloud gather on their personal horizon, then they feel betrayed, their belief has been splintered.

There are others however, for whom faith becomes a stimulant to heroic responses to the severest challenges of adversity. They do not expect God to keep them from trouble but rather to enable them to accept it when necessary and surmount it when possible.

A little while ago, I heard a radio address delivered by a man who had lost both legs and had gone on to create for himself a useful career at the head of an organization called "Abilities Incorporated." This organization employs only handicapped people. After the speaker told how he had learned to go on despite his own handicap, he concluded with the following declamation written by another but which he had adopted for himself:

> I asked God for strength, that I might achieve,
> I was made weak, that I might learn humbly to
> obey. . . .
> I asked for health, that I might do greater things,
> I was given infirmity, that I might do better things. . . .
> I asked for riches, that I might be happy,
> I was given poverty that I might be wise. . . .
> I asked for power, that I might have the praise of men,
> I was given weakness, that I might feel the need of
> God . . .
> I asked for all things, that I might enjoy life,
> I was given life, that I might enjoy all things. . . .
> I got nothing that I asked for—but everything I had
> hoped for,
> Almost despite myself, my unspoken prayers were
> answered.
> I am among all men, most richly blessed.

That man, dear friends, had made of God the vital center in his life in the time of trouble.

But life as we know is not only a series of burdens. It also has its great hours of achievement and success. As the prayer reminds us, IF can also be a series of pleasant possibilities—

> Who shall live?
> Who shall have rest?
> Who shall be tranquil?
> Who shall be at ease?
> Who shall wax rich?
> Who shall be exalted?

What does it mean to put God at the center of life in the time of triumph?

Well, at first blush, this problem doesn't seem quite so pressing. When we are well and prosperous we can manage quite well ourselves, thank you. A solvent business-man rarely advertises for partners.

On second glance, however, we notice that the prosperous man is not always the happy man. Success in any field does not necessarily bring the fulfilment it promises. Someone has reversed the popular slogan, "Nothing succeeds like success," to make it say: "Nothing fails like success." This revised version contains a genuine psychological insight. For it is only after we succeed in attaining any material goal that we realize that by itself it can never bring happiness. Those of us who are today earning what appeared to us in our lean college days astronomical figures, are we basically happier than we were then? Is there necessarily more contentment in the modern well-appointed split-level home than there was in the unfurnished flat in which the marriage began? Is it merely a coincidence that the Age of Anxiety has coincided with the Age of Abundance or is it true as Tolstoy said that discontent is not the result of man's needs but of man's abundance? The Psalmist spoke of an affliction God sometimes visits upon the successful: "And He gave them what they asked for but He sent a hunger into their souls."

To put God at the center of life in the time of triumph means to recognize that basically we are spiritual creatures and no matter how we pamper our bodies it shall avail us not at all unless we also nourish our souls. And it means something else too—something a famous rabbi once taught a former pupil.

The pupil of the Chafetz Chayim had ventured forth from the Yeshiva, gone to a distant town, and prospered in the business world. Some years later, the rabbi was passing through this town and naturally the business man came to visit his teacher.

"What are you doing?" the rabbi asked solicitously.

"Thank you," his pupil answered, "I'm doing quite well. My

243

business has grown, I have many employees, my financial rating is very high."

The conversation turned to other matters. In a little while the rabbi asked again: "What are you doing?"

It seemed strange that the rabbi should repeat the question he had already answered. But the rabbi was growing older. His memory apparently was not what it used to be.

"Thank you," the pupil said a second time, "I have a nice family, a lovely wife and fine children who are growing beautifully."

Again the conversation drifted into other channels. After they had roamed over a variety of subjects, the rabbi asked a third time:

"What are you doing?"

This time the pupil could not longer contain himself. "Rabbi," he protested, "you have already asked this very question three times!"

"Yes, my son" the rabbi said in mild rebuke. "I have asked three times but you have not answered the question even once. I have asked 'What are you doing?' You tell me of your prosperity, your family. That's not your doing. That is God's doing. I asked you what are you doing? How much charity are you giving? What are you doing for your people? Now tell me, my son, what are you doing? Vos tust du?"

To make God the vital center of our lives in the hour of triumph means to regard ourselves under obligation to return to Him a portion of the physical and financial means with which He has blessed us.

For last I have left what I consider to be the supreme significance of making God the vital center of our lives. To do so, is not only to arm us with a strategy of action for any specific life situation. To put God in the middle of life means to make the whole enterprise, the whole business of life meaningful. Unless

God is at work at the very core of life, what sense does the whole thing make?

Basically, the anxiety of our time derives in profound measure not so much from the uncertainty as to what life will bring us, as from the uncertainty as to what life means. Is life worthwhile? Does it have any intrinsic value?

We find evidence of this groping in least expected places. Let John Steinbeck in his book "Sweet Thursday" bear testimony. "Where does discontent start?" he asks. "You are warm enough but you shiver. You are fed, yet hunger gnaws you. You have been loved, but your yearning wanders in new fields. And to prod all these, there's time. . . . The end of life is now not so terribly far away—you can see it the way you see the finish line when you come into the stretch, and your mind says: 'What has my life meant so far, and what can it mean in the time left to me? What have I contributed to the Great Ledger? What am I worth?' "

Not all of us are as articulate as Steinbeck but isn't he really giving voice to the most crucial questions which agitate us? "What has my life meant so far? What can it mean? What am I worth?"

Those who have discarded a belief in God will give us no comforting answers. You and I are here for no conceivable purpose, going nowhere in particular on a journey which is full of sound and fury but signifies absolutely nothing. You and I are, as one of them put it, "only a bundle of cellular matter on its way to becoming manure," and life, in the words of another, "is a nightmare between two nothings." This is one set of answers we can give Steinbeck's piercing questions.

But when God becomes the vital center of our lives, we get an entirely different set of answers. Your life and mine become infinitely precious because there is a spark of divinity aglow within us. "Each one of us is a priceless bit of mosaic in the design of God's universe." We are but little lower than the angels. We are here at God's orders rendering a command performance. And what we do with our lives is of everlasting significance. Life is an unending adventure towards the goal of becoming human.

Zochraynu l'chayim melech chofetz b'chayim, "Remember us to life O King because You want us to live."

The cyclone of which we spoke at the beginning derives its extraordinary driving power because as the poet said, in its heart "is a place of central calm." If we are to live our lives with courage, with compassion and with conviction we need God in our hearts to give our lives a place of central calm.

"And I said to the man who stood at the gate to the year: 'Give me a light that I may tread safely into the unknown.'

And he replied:

Go out into the darkness and put your hand into the Hand of God.

That shall be to you better than light and safer than a known way!"

(*M. Louise Haskins*)

THE ART OF FORGIVENESS

In one of his short stories, Leo Tolstoy came to grips with one of life's most intimate and fundamental themes—a theme which is at the very core of Yom Kippur. Both the writer and the day urge us to master a difficult but desperately needed art—the art of forgiving.

Preached on Yom Kippur, 1958

22

The Art of Forgiveness

DEATH IS A great democrat. In his eyes we are all equal. In his presence our human oneness is dramatically underscored. We are bound to one another by the awareness of the common ravage to which we are all heir. Thus this *Yizkor* moment finds us more than a congregation. We are a closely-knit human family.

The atmosphere of comradeship and brotherhood which prevails at this hour is conducive to discussing an intimate problem of the human heart. How can we cultivate the fine art of forgiveness?

That there is an overwhelming need for us to learn this difficult art is borne in upon me with ever-increasing forcefulness from day to day. So many of us are walking around carrying mountains of resentments and harboring a multitude of festering angers, grudges and hates.

I am preparing to conduct a funeral service and the undertaker says: "We will cut *k'riyah* for the children separately and for the brothers separately. It is best not to bring them together." Or I ask for the address where the Shiva will be observed and after an embarrassed silence I am informed that it is better not to announce any address because the so called "family" will not be sitting together. Two daughters are shedding copious tears before the final service for their mother and one interrupts her lament to lash out at the other: "Now you are here to cry. Where were you when Mama was alive?" These are not imaginary situations. They are brutally real.

249

The resentments which like sticky scum come to the surface on the sea of sorrow are miserable components of too many lives. They are alienating parents from children and children from parents. They are erecting ever taller walls between husbands and wives and wives and husbands. They splinter families and shatter friendships. They add an icy breath to an already frigid society.

That is why I want to discuss this problem today when we are huddled together for a little extra warmth in the chilly presence of death. And the central theme of Yom Kippur, the day of forgiveness, is an eminently suitable backdrop against which we should think of this matter. To be sure there is a vital difference. On Yom Kippur we beg for God's forgiveness. What I am asking is that we think instead of granting forgiveness to one another. These two dimensions of forgiveness are not unrelated. We cannot solicit forgiveness unless we practice it. We cannot even believe that God forgives unless we can feel the power to do likewise. We cannot merit God's forgiveness for ourselves unless we are capable of extending it to others. "Forgive your neighbor," urges Ben Sira, "and then when you pray your sins will be forgiven."

This advice is easy to dispense but it is excruciatingly difficult to follow, isn't it? We have been bruised and hurt, we have been slighted and slandered, we have been outraged and offended, we have been publicly embarrassed and humiliated, our words have been distorted and our motives have been impugned, our reputations have been tarnished and our characters tainted. Whose ego is immune to any one or to a combination of such lacerations in the course of time? The most natural reaction, the primitive animal reaction, is to strike back ferociously or, if that is not immediately possible, to take refuge in thoughts of sweet revenge. A host of defiant battle slogans come tramping into our resentful hearts through the open wound. "So I'm not good enough for her!" "I'll teach him a lesson he'll never forget!" "I'm going to let him have it in spades!" As children we were content to return a blow for a blow and get even. Now we intend to return two for one and make profit.

Thus, we magnify our hurts, we dwell upon them, nurse them along and watch them grow until they fill our whole insides.

But do we ever stop to think that revenge is not only sweet, it is also exorbitantly costly? Do we pause to calculate the frightfully high price-tag affixed to our hatreds and our unevened scores?

One of the most gripping of Tolstoy's short stories drives home this point with unforgettable emphasis. It concerns two peasants, Ivan and Gabriel, whose farms bordered each other and whose families had lived in true neighborly fashion for several generations. But then there was a trivial misunderstanding between Ivan's daughter-in-law and Gabriel's mother. It started, of all things, over a hen's egg. One harsh word led to an accusing rebuke. Names began to fly and soon fists, hair was plucked and shirts were torn. Thus, the feud was started and like an unchecked cancerous growth it spread.

Ivan's invalid old father who lived with him tried to make peace: "It's a stupid thing," he told his children, "picking quarrels about such a paltry matter. Just think! The whole thing began over an egg. . . . What's the value of one egg. God sends enough for all! And suppose your neighbor did say an unkind word—put it right! Show her how to say a better one! If you nurse your anger it will be worse for you yourselves."

But they do not listen to the old man. The feud instead of subsiding keeps gathering momentum. At last, Ivan enjoys a huge measure of revenge. He hauls Gabriel before the District Court on a charge of having inflicted a blow upon his pregnant daughter-in-law, who had in fact first shamed Gabriel at a wedding by publicly calling him a horse thief. By bribing an elder of the court,

Ivan succeeds in obtaining a verdict against Gabriel. He receives twenty lashes with a birch rod.

Ivan's satisfaction was to prove extremely brief. That night, as he is nervously surveying his estate he sees the crouching figure of Gabriel lighting a bunch of straw under the eaves on his property. "Ah," thought Ivan, "now he won't escape! I'll catch him in the act!" And so instead of trying to stamp out the fire he runs in pursuit of Gabriel. He is almost upon him in the darkness when Gabriel fells him with a stunning blow of an oak wedge over his head.

When Ivan comes to, it looks like daylight. The raging fire which lights up the black night consumes Ivan's home, and Gabriel's home and half the village. Ivan's father soon dies as a result of burns he suffers in the conflagration. All Ivan can do is mutter dazedly: "What is this, friends? Why, all I had to do was snatch it out from under the eaves and trample on it! What is this, friends?"

Tolstoy named this story, "A Spark Neglected Burns the House."

Far-fetched? Fiction? Fantasy? Not necessarily. Extreme perhaps, but lifted straight out of our human stupidity. It is a bitter truth that countless lives are unnecessarily distorted and twisted by unresolved enmities. Lewis E. Lawes, the former warden of Sing Sing prison, once declared that our prisons are filled with people who could not or would not forget. More of us than we care to admit live in self-made dungeons behind bars erected by our resentments.

There are also more subtle ways that we pay for our inability to forgive than Ivan and Gabriel did. There are a variety of hidden charges. For one thing, when we allow our hatreds to clot and coagulate they are very prone to take a heavy toll on our health, our serenity, our efficiency. "Hatred," someone has correctly observed, "is a precious liquor . . . because it is made of

252

our blood, our health, our sleep and two thirds of our love." Our hatreds hurt us far more than they do those whom we hate. There are actual medical studies which prove that resentment causes such diverse ailments as indigestion, excessive tiredness, headaches and high blood pressure. Is any hatred worth that much?

We also shrink in moral stature when we permit our memories to be poisoned and cluttered up with irritating remembrances. They invariably bring out our least attractive qualities. They unloose a whole train of ugly traits. That is why Booker T. Washington, the great Negro inventor, was so wise when he said: "I am determined to permit no man to narrow or degrade my soul by making me hate him." And so when the Torah urges us: Lo tikom velo titor, "Thou shalt not take vengeance nor bear any grudge," it is actually laying down not only a high ethical principle, it is also giving us a prescription against physical and moral deterioration. Rabbi Asher ben Yechiel who lived in the fourteenth century put the matter more concretely: "Each night before retiring forgive anyone who may have offended you."

How then are we to cultivate the fine and difficult art of forgiveness?

The first quality that we need, it seems to me, is a generous degree of imagination, the capacity to project ourselves sympathetically into the position of the offender. Why did he do what he did? Why did she say what she did? What was bothering him? What was eating her? We know our own fears and frustrations, our deeply imbedded weakness and inadequacies, our besetting anxieties and haunting failures. We know these things and we make allowances for them—in ourselves. Are we as prone to try to understand them and to make allowances for them in others?

The housewife after a weary day at home when her nerves are raw and exposed is quick to make excuses for her own edgy remarks and biting criticisms. Is she as likely to try to understand that her husband's impatient and uncharitable observations may also be occasioned by a thousand pin-pricks he suffered on his job that day trying to keep the home going? The well-known story may be apocryphal but there is genuine psychological insight in the taunt of the wife who greets her husband at the end of the day with: "Here I am sweating all day in the hot kitchen while you enjoy your job in a nice cool sewer."

The heart knows its own anguish but does it attempt to feel the anguish in the heart of another? The bully who tramples upon our sensitivities is not an easy person to take but our charged feelings against him could be greatly assuaged if we try to understand that his aggressive exterior may only be a mask behind which he is trying to conceal a haunting sense of inferiority. The gossip who stains our fair name has robbed us of something infinitely precious but when we begin to understand that gossip so often represents a desperate craving to be listened to or an attempt to project onto others a fault which weighs heavily on one's own conscience, our indignation more readily gives way to pity.

A French saying tells us that, *Tout comprendre, c'est tout pardonner*, to understand all is to forgive all. When we stop short of forgiveness, it is in no small measure due to our own refusal through imagination to make the effort to understand. To imagine means to present an image, a picture, to ourselves. The more complete our picture of the one who has wronged us, the more we know of the parents who reared him, the early environment which molded him, the bruises which scarred him, the dreams which were denied him—the more complete the picture, the more total our understanding, the more likely our forgiveness.

But, we will protest, who can indeed know that much about another? Why we scarcely know that much about ourselves! That is precisely so and that leads me to the second quality we need for the fine art of forgiving—humility.

We recall that when Jacob dies, Joseph's brothers grow fearful that Joseph will now avenge himself for the wrongs they perpetrated against him. They therefore plead with him to forgive their sins. And Joseph reassures them with a remarkable sentence: "Do not fear for am I in the place of God?" This is a crucial question that each of us should put to himself. Am I indeed in the place of God? Who am I to pass judgment on my fellow man? I who see so little and understand less, am I equipped with sufficient perception, insight and wisdom to be judge and jury over another? We urgently need a saving sense of humility to keep us from committing the cardinal blasphemy of impersonating God. Justice Holmes who by virtue of his office did have to sit in judgment on others, once wrote to the philosopher William James: "The great act of faith is when a man decides he is not God." Being somewhat less than God and having to rely upon defective vision and restricted faculties, it is far more becoming to forgive than to condemn.

Humility does something more for us too. It prompts us to focus less attention on the offences of others and more upon our own. To be sure I suffered hurt but did I not also inflict it? If there was a breach in the family relationship, how much of it was of my doing? Ivan's father in Tolstoy's story, makes this very point when he pleads with him to bear no malice against Gabriel: "Others' sins are before your eyes but your own are behind your back. You say he's acted badly. What a thing to say! If he were the only one to act badly, how could strife exist? Is strife among men ever bred by one alone? Strife is always between two. His badness you see but your own you don't. If he were bad, but you were good, there would be no strife."

But Ivan, as we know, was too proud to admit his share in precipitating the quarrel. It is only after the destructive fire that the awful truth dawns upon him. His dying father asks him: "Who has burnt down the village?"

"It was he, father! I caught him in the act. I saw him shove the firebrand into the thatch. I might have pulled away the burning straw and stamped it out, and then nothing would have happened."

"Ivan," said the old man, "I am dying and you in your turn will have to face death. Whose is the sin?"

For a while Ivan was silent. His father repeated the question: "Now before God, say whose is the sin?"

"Mine, father!" And he fell on his knees begging: "Forgive me, father; I am guilty before you and before God."

Thus in the agonizing soul-searching of a man who paid a terribly exorbitant price for his inability to forgive, Ivan at last confesses that he too shared in Gabriel's sin. Humbled by compound tragedy, Ivan realizes the burning truth of his father's words which he had earlier spurned: "Is strife ever bred by one alone?"

It takes humility to beg forgiveness. It requires humility to grant it.

Lastly, I would suggest, that the art of forgiveness requires a capacity to feel compassion. Compassion, I would define as your pain in my heart. What a crying need this world has for compassion. How hungry we all are for it. Is there any among us so rich that he can do without love? Is there any so poor that he cannot give it? And, as the Bible reminds us, love is the best thing with which to cover wrongs.

A mother whose son had taken to evil ways asked the Baal Shem Tov what she should do. And The Master of the Good Name answered: "Love him all the more."

Hearts which have been hardened by hatreds, can be softened by more love. Memories which have been cluttered up by grudges can be swept clean by more love. Minds which have been imprisoned by resentments can be liberated by more love.

At Yizkor time we become poignantly aware of how little time we have to love each other. Life is too short to be little. Christopher Morley once said that, "If we were given five minutes' warning before sudden death, five minutes to say what it had all meant to us, every telephone booth would be occupied by people trying to call up other people to stammer that they loved them." Well, life does not always take the trouble to sound the alarm. Must we therefore live as though we had all eternity for love, all eternity for forgiveness? "Remember thy latter end and cease from enmity."

Our compassion is kindled by our need for giving love and for tasting it. It is kindled too by our realization, especially vivid at this *Yizkor* hour, that there is in life enough anguish and heart-break, enough suffering and agony without our adding to the sum.

> "My heart was heavy, for its trust had been
> Abused, its kindness answered with foul wrong;
> So, turning gloomily from my fellowmen,
> One summer Sabbath day I strolled among
> The green mounds of the village burial-place;
> Where pondering how all human love and hate
> Find one sad level; and how, soon or late,
> Wronged and wrongdoer, each with meekened face,
> And cold hands folded over a still heart,
> Pass the green threshold of our common grave,
> Whither all footsteps tend, whence none depart,
> Awed for myself, and pitying my race,
> Our common sorrow, like a mighty wave
> Swept all my pride away, and trembling I forgave!"
>
> (*John Greenleaf Whittier*)

We all need to forgive no less than we all need to be forgiven. "For the sin which we have sinned before Thee, *biyodim uvlo yodim*, consciously and unconsciously." We hurt without meaning to. Those we love most we are prone to hurt most because our lives intersect at more points. Let this hour move us to imitate Him to whom we pray so that we may merit the Divine assurance: *Vayomer Adonoy solachti kidvorecha*—"And the Lord said: I have forgiven according to thy word." As we speak the words "I forgive," God will respond "I forgive."

Temple Israel
Minneapolis, Minnesota

IN HONOR OF
THE SPEEDY RECOVERY OF
DR. PAUL SLATON
FROM
GEORGIA & IVAN KALMAN